MEDITERRANEAN, KETO AND VEGAN

COOKBOOK

ISBN

9798496987141

Sharma

Legal & Disclaimer

The information contained in this book and its contents is not designed to replace or take the place of any form of medical or professional advice; and is not meant to replace the need for independent medical, financial, legal or other professional advice or services, as may be required. The content and information in this book has been provided for educational and entertainment purposes only.

The content and information contained in this book has been compiled from sources deemed reliable, and it is accurate to the best of the Author's knowledge, information and belief. However, the Author cannot guarantee its accuracy and validity and cannot be held liable for any errors and/or omissions. Further, changes are periodically made to this book as and when needed. Where appropriate and/or necessary, you must consult a professional (including but not limited to your doctor, attorney, financial advisor or such other professional advisor) before using any

TABLE OF CONTENTS

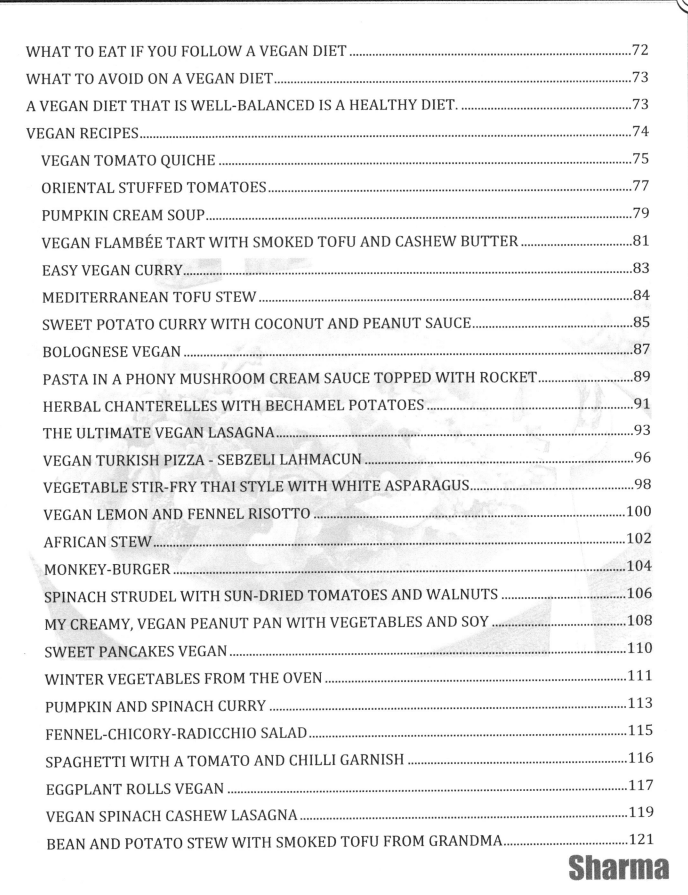

Sharma

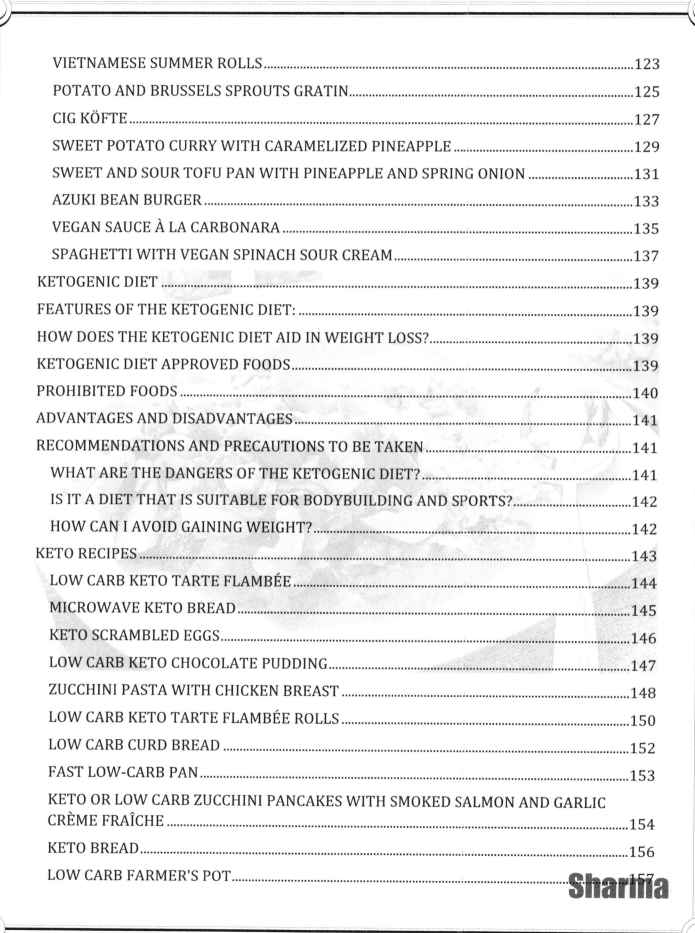

Sharma

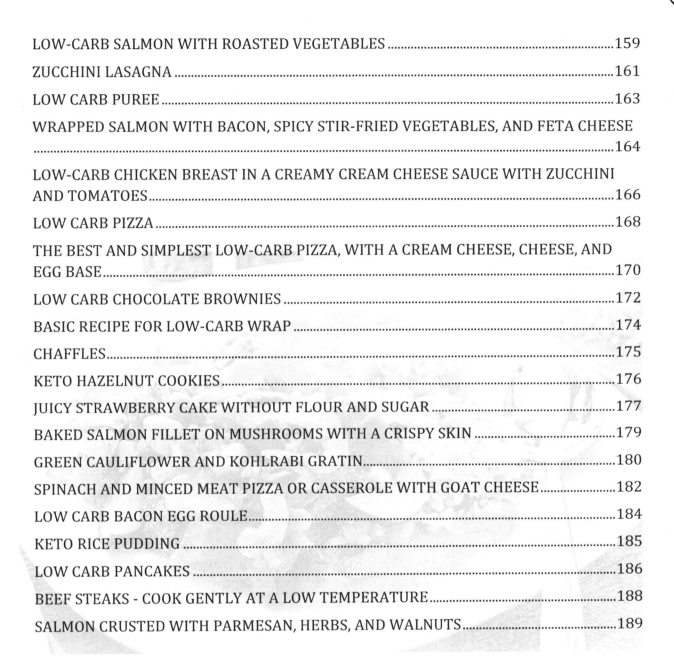

Sharma

MEDITERRANEAN DIET

The aim of the Mediterranean diet is to extend life expectancy by protecting against cardiovascular diseases as well as cancer risks. It is directly inspired by the traditional eating habits of the Mediterranean rim's populations. It encourages the consumption of plants, good fats, and whole grains. Red meat, sugar, and industrial products, on the other hand, have a very limited place.

CHARACTERISTICS OF THE MEDITERRANEAN DIET:

- ❖ Protector against cardiovascular disease and certain cancers
- ❖ Based on a predominantly vegetable diet
- ❖ Rich in quality unsaturated fats
- ❖ Exceptional intake of fiber, antioxidants and vitamins
- ❖ Weight loss is not a priority

THE MAIN PRINCIPLES OF THE REGIME

Ancel Keys conducted a scientific study in the 1950s that revealed that the populations of Crete and Corfu had a higher life expectancy despite having a rudimentary health system. In the 1990s, Dr. Serge Renaud's "French paradox" highlighted the link between the Mediterranean diet and a low rate of recurrence of cardiovascular disease.

HOW DOES THE MEDITERRANEAN DIET WORK?

The Mediterranean diet's goal is not to lose weight, but to maintain arterial health in order to prevent cardiovascular disease and to lower the risk of contracting cancer. Despite the fact that the frequency of consumption of fatty, sweet, and processed foods is low, this often results in weight loss.

HOW DOES THE MEDITERRANEAN DIET HELP YOU LOSE WEIGHT?

The Mediterranean diet, with its interesting content of monounsaturated fatty acids (from olive oil) and a small amount of saturated fatty acids (from fatty meat), helps reduce cholesterol levels as well as atherosclerosis. In addition, fruits and vegetables as well as red wine containing tannins are believed to provide an excellent source of antioxidants that help protect against diseases associated with aging. These effects, however, are seen in people who engage in regular physical activity, so it is critical to combine this diet with an active lifestyle to reap the benefits.

This diet's primary goal is not to lose weight. However, it is natural to lose weight in the first few weeks after starting a healthy diet free of sugary, industrial products, and bad fats. All the more so if the diet was previously anarchic and unbalanced.

HOW LONG DOES THE MEDITERRANEAN DIET LAST?

The Mediterranean diet does not have a time limit. The health benefits, and in particular the prevention of cardiovascular disease, are observed in the long term. Rather, it is a way of life that should inspire us to make better food choices every day.

FOODS PERMITTED IN THE CRETAN DIET, AS WELL AS FREQUENCY OF CONSUMPTION

The following are the different food categories and the frequency with which they are consumed in the Mediterranean diet:

- ❖ Abundance of whole grain products
- ❖ Abundance of fruits and vegetables
- ❖ Plenty of garlic, onion, spices and herbs
- ❖ Use of olive and rapeseed oil as fatty substance
- ❖ Daily consumption of legumes, nuts and seeds
- ❖ Yogurt and sheep cheese are consumed on a daily basis (but no milk)
- ❖ Consumption of red wine on a daily basis, but in moderation (12 cl/day)
- ❖ Fish consumption is high (several times a week)
- ❖ Consumption of chicken and eggs is restricted (a few times a week)
- ❖ Sugary foods should be consumed in moderation (a few times a week)
- ❖ Red meat consumption is extremely low (a few times a month)

Calorie intake that is reasonable on a daily basis (1,800 to 2,500 calories per day depending on physical activity)

ADVANTAGES AND DISADVANTAGES

THE POSITIVE POINTS OF THE MEDITERRANEAN DIET

- ❖ Excellent supply of quality fatty acids
- ❖ Rich in micronutrients, antioxidants and dietary fiber
- ❖ Protection against cellular aging and cardiovascular disease
- ❖ No frustration or monotony
- ❖ Easy to follow
- ❖ Compatible with an active social life
- ❖ Satiety provided by fiber and vegetable proteins

- ❖ Decrease in food quality
- ❖ Requires an effort of cultural adaptation
- ❖ May be difficult for heavy red meat eaters to follow
- ❖ Requires some cooking

RECOMMENDATIONS AND PRECAUTIONS TO BE TAKEN

ARE THERE ANY RISKS?

As soon as the Mediterranean diet is adapted to the needs of the body, then there is no risk in following it. On the contrary, it is a varied and balanced diet rich in high-quality micro and macronutrients.

IS THIS A DIET FOR YOU?

Yes, if you want to protect your cardiovascular system and live a long and healthy life. It is all the more indicated if you suffer from lipid balance disorders (hypercholesterolemia, hypertriglyceridemia, etc.), from a metabolic syndrome or from a history of cardiovascular pathologies. If you are overweight, the Mediterranean diet can also be a great way to achieve a healthy weight. If you are already in good health, the Cretan diet will help you keep it that way for as long as possible.

IS IT A DIET COMPATIBLE WITH SPORT?

Absolutely, physical activity is one of the pillars of the Mediterranean diet. A. Keys discovered that gentle physical activity in the open air was an essential part of everyday life by studying the populations of the Mediterranean rim. To maximize the effects of the Mediterranean diet, it is recommended to engage in 30 minutes of physical activity per day, such as walking, hiking, cycling, running, swimming, dancing, and so on.

DIETICIAN'S THOUGHTS ON THE MEDITERRANEAN DIET

The Mediterranean diet is a great source of inspiration for healthy eating on a daily basis without giving in to the call of restrictive diets. It provides guidelines for a balanced diet and is simple to follow for those who are used to cooking and enjoy the flavors of southern cuisine. It aids in the preservation of the cardiovascular system as well as the attainment and maintenance of a healthy weight. I can only recommend to follow the main principles of the Cretan diet on a daily basis, to be and stay in full health.

MEDITERRANEAN RECIPES

MEDITERRANEAN PUMPKIN SOUP

Preparation time: 20 minutes

Cooking/Baking time: 50 minutes

Serving: 4

INGREDIENTS

- 750 g Pumpkin (se) with shell (e.g. Hokkaido)
- 6th Tomatoes)
- 1 Onion (noun)
- 4th Garlic cloves)
- 4 branch / s   Rosemary, fresh
- salt and pepper
- 4 tbsp olive oil
- 500 ml Vegetable broth
- 75 g Olives, black, pitted
- Parmesan, coarsely grated

PREPARATION

1. Preheat the oven to 220 ° C. Halve, core and cut the pumpkin into pieces. Wash tomatoes and cut in half. Peel the onion and cut into rings. Peel the garlic cloves.
2. Put the vegetables in an ovenproof dish and sprinkle the rosemary sprigs on top. Salt generously and sprinkle with fresh pepper from the mill. Drizzle with olive oil

and roast in the preheated oven for about 50 minutes. Then let it cool down and remove the rosemary.

3. Bring the vegetable stock to the boil. Add the vegetables and purée finely with a hand blender. This creates a creamy, thick soup.

4. Chop the olives and add them. Reheat the soup and arrange on plates. Sprinkle with coarsely grated parmesan and serve. It is best to serve with white bread.

MEDITERRANEAN BAKED SWEET POTATOES WITH ROASTED CHICKPEAS

Preparation time: 5 minutes

Cooking/Baking time: 25 minutes

Serving: 4

INGREDIENTS

- 600 g Sweet potato
- 425 g Canned chickpeas
- ½ tbsp Coriander powder, ground
- ½ tbsp Ground cumin powder
- ½ tbsp Paprika powder, optionally smoked
- 1 Lemon (s), untreated
- 60 g Hummus
- 3 tbsp dill
- 3 toe / n Garlic, chopped
- Almond milk (almond drink), unsweetened, alternatively water
- 50 g Cherry tomato (s), diced
- 20 g Parsley, chopped
- Chili sauce with garlic
-

PREPARATION

1. Preheat the oven to 200 ° C. Wash the potatoes and cut them in half lengthways. You can also leave the potatoes whole, but this increases the baking time to around 45 minutes to 1 hour.
2. Drain and dry the chickpeas and mix with the olive oil and the spices (coriander, cumin, paprika) and place on a baking sheet lined with baking paper.
3. Rub the potatoes with olive oil, lightly salt and then place with the cut surface facing down on the same baking sheet as the chickpeas. Depending on the size of the baking tray, it may be necessary to use a separate one for the potatoes.
4. Put the potatoes and chickpeas in the oven for about 25 minutes.
5. While the potatoes and chickpeas are roasting in the oven, prepare the sauce. To do this, mix the hummus with the dill, the juice of half a lemon and the chopped garlic cloves in a bowl and dilute with the almond milk or water so that you can later pour the sauce over the potatoes. Now season with salt, pepper and the spices you used.
6. Now prepare the parsley and tomato topping. Mix the diced tomatoes with the parsley, a little lemon juice and a little of the chilli sauce and set aside for a moment so that the whole thing can go through a bit.
7. If you don't have a chilli-garlic sauce, you can just use chilli powder or fresh and a little garlic.
8. Once the chickpeas are golden brown and the sweet potatoes are tender, remove them from the oven.
9. Place the sweet potatoes on the plates with the cut side up and mash the potato meat a little with a fork. Put the chickpeas on top and pour the hummus sauce over them. Garnish with the tomato topping. Serve hot immediately.

MEDITERRANEAN STIR-FRY VEGETABLES WITH CHICKEN BREAST FILLET

Preparation time: 30 minutes

Cooking/Baking time: 40 minutes

Serving: 4

INGREDIENTS

- 600 g   Chicken breast fillet (s)
- 2 Tea spoons olive oil
- 250 ml Vegetable broth
- 1 m large Onion (noun)
- 2 Garlic cloves)
- 2 Bell pepper (s), red (or 1 red and 1 yellow)
- 150 g zucchini
- 100 g Carrot
- 200 g Mushrooms, fresh
- 200 g sour cream
- 75 g Creme fraiche Cheese
- 1 glass Red wine, drier (omit in children)
- Basil, frozen or fresh
- 6 branch / s   thyme

- n. B Herbs, Italian
- n. B Chilli pepper (s), dried
- salt and pepper
- n. B Rosemary, fresh or dried

PREPARATION

1. Dice the chicken. Clean the peppers and carrots and also cut them into cubes or bite-sized pieces. Peel the garlic and onion and chop finely (do not press the garlic). Wash the zucchini and cut into thin slices, also cut the mushrooms into slices.

2. Heat the olive oil in a wok (alternatively also a pot) and fry the diced chicken (not too hot) with a little rosemary and a little paprika powder until it has a brownish crust. Remove the meat and, if necessary, keep it warm (but not necessary).

3. Pour fresh oil into the pot or wok and gradually add the vegetables. The following sequence has worked well for me: onions, garlic (only briefly, as the garlic burns easily), carrots, mushrooms, peppers and zucchini. Fry everything for about 10 minutes before deglazing with 250 mL vegetable stock. Combine the sour cream, crème fraîche, and a splash of red wine in a mixing bowl. Season with Italian herbs, paprika powder, chili peppers, pepper, and salt to taste (be careful, as the broth already has a lot of salt).

4. Add the meat again. Add some basil, place the thyme sprigs on top and leave everything with the lid closed on a low heat for about 20 minutes. Take out the thyme sprigs and season again to taste. If necessary, thicken with a little sauce thickener for light sauce. I recommend rice with this. But it is certainly also very tasty with other side dishes.

SUMMER GRILLED PEPPERS WITH A MEDITERRANEAN FILLING FROM ILLES

Preparation time: 20 minutes

Cooking/Baking time: 20 minutes

Serving: 2

INGREDIENTS

- 3 Bell pepper (s), red, yellow, green
- 1 teaspoon Olive oil, for spraying
- 2 m large Onion (noun)
- 1 Garlic cloves)
- Sea salt, possibly ground with thyme
- pepper

FOR THE FILLING:

- 200 g Ricotta or low-fat quark
- 60 g Sheep cheese light, crumbled
- 50 g Olives, chopped, green or black of your choice
- 1 teaspoon olive oil
- 1 small Garlic cloves)
- Spice (s), Mediterranean, ground

- salt and pepper
- Herbs, fresh such as parsley, dill, chives, basil
- 1 slice / n Grilled cheese per filled bell pepper, optional

PREPARATION

1. Since my dishes are suitable for ww-g, the ingredients such as sheep's cheese, oil and olives can be adapted or increased at any time to your own needs!
2. Fill the pepper halves with onion slices cut lengthwise! Season with the sea salt / thyme mixture and pepper and drizzle with oil! Grill for 10 - 15 minutes in the microwave; if you prefer it softer, grill for 5 minutes longer. (In the oven, it may take a little longer!) The peppers should not turn black because they should not be peeled, but rather slightly over-grilled!
3. Season with salt and pepper to taste after mixing the quark with the other ingredients. Allow the peppers to cool before filling with the quark mixture (about 50 g per half pepper)! Serve with toasted bread or grilled potatoes!

Preparation time: 30 minutes

Cooking/Baking time: 50 minutes

Serving: 4

INGREDIENTS

- 800 ml fish stock
- 200 ml White wine, drier (e.g. Pinot Grigio)
- 100 g Onion (s), red, in strips
- 100 g Carrot (s) in strips
- 50 g Celery in strips
- 50 g Fennel in strips
- 100 g Bell pepper (s), red,, in strips
- 10 Cocktail tomatoes
- 2 toe / n garlic
- 100 ml olive oil
- 15 g Tomato paste
- 400 g Fish, diced (Mediterranean fish, also goes well with salmon and redfish, cheaper and easier to get)
- 100 g Prawn tails or surimi (much cheaper but not as tasty)
- salt and pepper

- Basil, fresh
- oregano
- thyme

PREPARATION

1. Sweat the vegetable strips in olive oil. Add the tomato paste and the finely chopped garlic cloves, deglaze with white wine and fill up with fish stock.
2. Cook until the vegetables are tender but still have a bit of bite to them. Add the fish and let it steep, season to taste and serve in deep pasta plates. To garnish, fry the cocktail tomatoes briefly in hot olive oil and add to the soup with fresh basil.

MEDITERRANEAN MASHED POTATOES

Preparation time: 20 minutes

Cooking/Baking time: 10 minutes

Serving: 4

INGREDIENTS

- 1 kg Potato (s), mainly waxy
- 4th Shallot (noun)
- 2 toe / n garlic
- 1 bunch basil
- 100 g Tomato (s), dried, pickled in oil
- 50 g Pine nuts
- 100 ml olive oil
- 1 teaspoon Lemon juice
- salt
- Pepper, freshly ground

PREPARATION

1. Peel the potato, wash and cook in salted water. Peel and finely dice shallots. Peel and thinly slice the garlic. Wash and pat dry the basil before plucking the leaves. Cut the tomatoes into pieces.
2. Dry-roast the pine nuts, then remove and set aside. Sauté the shallots and garlic in 2 tablespoons olive oil until translucent, then add the remaining oil and heat.

3. Drain the potatoes and mash them roughly with the oil. Season with salt and pepper and stir in the pine nuts, tomatoes, and basil. Top off with lemon juice.

Preparation time: 20 minutes

Cooking/Baking time: 20 minutes

Serving: 4

INGREDIENTS

- 300 g   Runner beans
- 250 g   Cherry tomato
- 200 g   Pasta
- 4 tbsp Parmesan, freshly grated
- 2 Garlic cloves)
- ½ cup Herbs, fresh, e.g. B. Savory, basil and chives
- 4 tbsp olive oil
- 1 tbsp Lemon juice
- salt and pepper
- Vegetable broth, grained
- 1 tbsp butter

PREPARATION

1. Wash the beans and cut them into bite-sized pieces after trimming the ends. Melt the butter in a large pan, add the beans and dust with the vegetable stock. Briefly sweat the beans, add approx. 100 ml of water and sauté for 15 minutes with the pan closed.
2. In the meantime, wash and halve the tomatoes and cook the pasta in salted water until al dente. Wash and finely chop the herbs, peel and chop the garlic cloves.
3. Mix the herbs, garlic, olive oil, and parmesan and lemon juice together. Season with salt and pepper.
4. Add the tomatoes to the beans and cook for another 5 minutes. Then mix the herb mixture and the cooked noodles into the beans, let them steep briefly and season with salt and pepper.

Preparation time: 20 minutes

Cooking/Baking time: 20 minutes

Serving: 4

INGREDIENTS

- 3 kg Mussel
- 2 tbsp Olive oil, good
- 4 toe / n Garlic, fresh
- 1 small Onion (noun)
- 1 stick / n leek
- 1 small Carrot
- ½ fret Parsley, smooth
- ½ Red pepper (s)
- 2 large can / n Tomatoes)
- some Herbs, fresh ital.
- some salt and pepper
- Possibly. Chilli pepper

PREPARATION

1. First, thoroughly wash the mussels under cold running water and use a knife to remove the threads (mussel whiskers). Please do not use mussels that have been opened because they are spoiled.

2. Cut the leek, carrot, and half of the bell pepper into as small pieces as possible. Ideally, julienne right away. If you want it spicier, you can add half or whole chilli pods.
3. Also cut the onion into small cubes and clean the garlic cloves and press them through the garlic press.
4. In a large saucepan, heat the olive oil and fry the onion cubes and garlic until translucent. Then add the rest of the vegetables. Cut the cans of tomatoes into small pieces with a knife and remove any peel remains and stems.
5. In the meantime, pluck the parsley from the stalks and chop them into small pieces. Add the ready-to-cook mussels and cook briefly over high heat until they open. Then reduce the heat and simmer for another 5 to 10 minutes.
6. Add some Italian herbs at the very end and also the fresh parsley. Add a fresh baguette and just enjoy!

Preparation time: 20 minutes

Cooking/Baking time: 35 minutes

Serving: 2

INGREDIENTS

- 6 m large Potato (s), waxy, eighths
- 1 large Bell pepper (s), red, approx. 200 g
- 150 g Mushrooms, brown
- 1 small Zucchini, approx. 300 g
- 1 large Onion (s), red
- 2 toe / n garlic
- 50 g Tomato paste, 3-fold concentrated
- 50 ml water
- 50 ml olive oil
- 1 teaspoon, heaped salt
- 1 teaspoon Pepper, white, freshly ground
- 1 tbsp Thyme, fresh, chopped, or dried, then finely grated
- 1 tbsp Rosemary, fresh, chopped
- 1 teaspoon sugar
- 1 tsp, leveled Harissa
- some Lemon zest, grated
- n. B Parmesan

PREPARATION

1. Wash the potatoes thoroughly, brush them off if necessary, dry them and cut them into eighths. Wash the peppers and zucchini, brush off the mushrooms, peel the garlic and onion.
2. Clean the peppers, sixths and cut into strips, halve the zucchini lengthways, then quarter and cut into pieces. Quarter the onion and cut into thin strips, quarter or sixth mushrooms depending on size, finely chop the garlic.
3. Mix the tomato paste with water, then with oil, spices, garlic and herbs. Mix the potatoes with half of the marinade and place in a baking dish in the oven at 170 to 180 degrees for 20 minutes, mix the remaining marinade with the vegetables.
4. Take the baking dish out again after approx. 20 minutes, add the marinated vegetables and mix with the potatoes. Place them in the oven for another 15 minutes. If you like, you can bake it with freshly grated Parmesan for a few minutes.

MEDITERRANEAN MINCED MEAT PUFF PASTRY SNAILS

Preparation time: 20 minutes

Cooking/Baking time: 20 minutes

Serving: 4

INGREDIENTS

- 275 g Puff pastry, fresh roll (or frozen)
- 500 g Minced meat
- 1 Red pepper (s)
- 1 half zucchini
- 150 g Tomato paste
- 2 ball / n Mozzarella
- 2 Shallot (noun)
- 5 toe / n garlic
- 2 Chilli pepper
- 1 shot Cream, (possibly)
- Basil, fresher
- Rosemary, fresher
- Thyme, fresher
- Oregano, fresher

PREPARATION

1. Cut the zucchini and bell pepper into small cubes. Cut the shallots, garlic, and chili pepper into small pieces. Chop the herbs into small pieces. Fry the minced meat with olive oil and remove. Sweat the paprika and zucchini in the mixture. Add shallots, garlic and chilli.
2. Then push the vegetables to the cooler edge of the pan and stir in the herbs. Lightly sweat the tomato paste in the hot zone. Add the minced meat again, season with salt and pepper. If you want, you can make it a little thicker with a dash of cream.
3. Allow it to cool before draining the accumulated oil. Ideally, let it steep for a day in the refrigerator.
4. Roll out the puff pastry and spread the mixture on top. Roll up the puff pastry with the mixture and press down the ends of the roll. Cut the roll into 2 cm slices and place it on a baking oven grate lined with baking paper with the cut side at the appropriate distance (open). Round the snails and cover with thin mozzarella slices.
5. Bake for about 20-25 minutes in a normal oven at 220 ° C to the desired golden tan. A clay bowl with water in the oven lets the snails rise nicely. Serve warm or cold.

Preparation time: 20 minutes

Cooking/Baking time: 20 minutes

Serving: 2

INGREDIENTS

- 2 Chicken breast fillet (s)
- 1 teaspoon olive oil
- 1 m large Onion (noun)
- 1 m large Garlic cloves)
- 1 Red pepper (s)
- 100 g zucchini
- 100 g Carrot
- 100 g Mushrooms
- 50 g sour cream
- 80 g Rice or pasta
- salt and pepper
- 1 pck Herbs, Italian, TK

PREPARATION

1. Bring the sun and the aroma of the Mediterranean into your home at your table. Low in fat and high in vegetables, this recipe is just right for a healthy diet.
2. Prepare rice or pasta according to the instructions on the packet. Clean and cut the vegetables into bite-sized pieces. Dice the chicken.
3. Heat the oil in a pan and fry the poultry. Gradually add the vegetables. Starting with onions, garlic, paprika, mushrooms, carrots and finally add the zucchini. Add a dash of water, cover the pan and simmer everything for about 10 minutes on a low heat.
4. Season with sour cream, salt, pepper and the Italian herbs and serve with pasta or rice.

MEDITERRANEAN CHICKEN BREAST FILLETS

Preparation time: 25 minutes

Cooking/Baking time: 25 minutes

Serving: 3

INGREDIENTS

- 3 port Chicken breast fillet (s)
- 6 slice / n Bacon
- 18th Olives, black, pitted
- 2 m large Onion (noun)
- 3 m large Tomato (s), (vine tomatoes, alternatively small tomatoes with firm flesh)
- 1 can Tomato (s), (pizza tomato)
- 3 Garlic cloves)
- 200 g   cream
- 200 g   Feta cheese, (sheep cheese)
- olive oil
- salt and pepper
- Paprika powder
- sugar
- 1 pck Herbs of Provence, TK

PREPARATION

1. Wash the chicken breast fillets, pat dry and season with a little salt, pepper and paprika. Wrap 2 bacon slices once over the long and short sides of each breast, making sure that the "locking points" are on top of each other.
2. Heat the olive oil in a pan and fry the fillets briefly and vigorously. Fry the side with the "locking point" first. Then put aside.
3. Fry a finely diced onion with the chopped garlic in the frying fat and deglaze with the pizza tomatoes and cream. Add a dash of olive oil, bring to the boil briefly and reduce to a creamy consistency. Season with salt, pepper, paprika and a pinch of sugar and add about half a pack of frozen herbs.
4. Grease a baking dish with a little olive oil and pour in the sauce. Place the chicken breasts inside. Cut the second onion into rings, quarter the tomatoes and spread the onions and tomatoes with the olives and the diced feta on the meat.
5. Sprinkle some more paprika powder and the rest of the herbs on top and bake at 200 degrees in the preheated oven for about 20 minutes. We like baguette or ciabatta best with it, because it sinks the sauce nicely.

Preparation time: 40 minutes

Cooking/Baking time: 1 hour 5 minutes

Serving: 4

INGREDIENTS

- 4th Fish fillet (s) (Pangasius, TK)
- 700 g Potatoes)
- 700 g zucchini
- 2 Red pepper (s)
- 1 Bell pepper (s), yellow
- 3 toe / n garlic
- 2 tbsp Palm fat (palmin)
- 250 g Tomatoes)
- 200 g Sheep cheese
- rosemary
- thyme
- salt and pepper
- ½ Lemon (s), the juice of it
- 4 tbsp Parmesan

PREPARATION

1. Thaw the frozen fish fillets and drizzle with lemon. Then season with salt and pepper in a baking dish.
2. Peel the potatoes, cut them into small cubes, and fry them in a pan with the Palmin until they are cooked, turning constantly (takes about 20 minutes). Meanwhile, clean and cut the zucchini and peppers into cubes.
3. Spread the fried potatoes with rosemary, thyme, salt, and pepper over the pangasius fillet. Now add the zucchini and pepper cubes to the pan and cook for 5 minutes. Squeeze the garlic cloves and season with salt and pepper.
4. Layer in the baking dish as well. Pour the sheep's cheese over the casserole. Roughly dice the tomatoes and place them in the gaps in the sheep's cheese. Now sprinkle with grated parmesan. Cook in a preheated oven at 190 ° C for about 40 minutes. Serve immediately.

MEDITERRANEAN NOODLE PAN WITH ZUCCHINI AND MUSHROOMS IN A DELICIOUS CREAM SAUCE

Preparation time: 20 minutes

Cooking/Baking time: 20 minutes

Serving: 4

INGREDIENTS

- 500 g Pasta
- 1 zucchini
- 250 g Mushrooms
- 2 Onion (noun)
- 250 g cream
- 2 toe / n garlic
- 1 Chilli pepper (s) or chilli powder
- 1 tbsp herbs of Provence
- Salt and pepper, black
- Paprika powder
- n. B olive oil

PREPARATION

1. Wash the zucchini and mushrooms. Cut the zucchini into small pieces and remove the stalks from the mushrooms. Cut these into small pieces. Cut the onions.

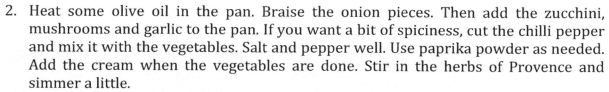

2. Heat some olive oil in the pan. Braise the onion pieces. Then add the zucchini, mushrooms and garlic to the pan. If you want a bit of spiciness, cut the chilli pepper and mix it with the vegetables. Salt and pepper well. Use paprika powder as needed. Add the cream when the vegetables are done. Stir in the herbs of Provence and simmer a little.

3. Put on pasta water. When the water boils, add the pasta to the water and cook until al dente or soft according to the instructions on the packet. Either mix the pasta into the sauce or put the pasta on the plate first and then pour the sauce over it.

4. A delicious tomato salad with balsamic cream and fresh shallots goes well with it.

Preparation time: 50 minutes

Cooking/Baking time: 3 minutes

Serving: 4

INGREDIENTS

- 750 g Shrimp (s) raw, headless with tail
- 2 Red hot peppers
- 6 toe / n garlic
- 2 branch / s   rosemary
- 10 sheets sage
- 10 tbsp Oil (olive oil)
- salt
- 4 tbsp Lemon juice
- 1 bunch Chopped parsley

PREPARATION

1. Thaw the prawns in the refrigerator in a colander, then wash in cold water and pat dry.
2. Remove the pepper's stem and all of the seeds. Peel and halve the garlic cloves. Heat olive oil in a pan. Place the prawns side by side and fry on each side for about 1 1/2 minutes over high heat.

3. After turning, add the garlic, hot peppers, sage and chopped rosemary. Salt everything, drizzle with lemon juice and mix in the parsley.

MEDITERRANEAN TURKEY ROLLS

Preparation time: 30 minutes

Cooking/Baking time: 20 minutes

Serving: 4

INGREDIENTS

- 4th Turkey schnitzel
- 125 g Mozzarella light
- 4 slice / n Ham, raw, max. 15% fat
- ¼ liter Vegetable broth
- 200 g Shallot (noun)
- 4th Tomatoes)
- 3 Garlic cloves)
- 1 teaspoon Tomato paste
- Pinch salt
- ½ tsp Black pepper, coarsely ground
- 1 teaspoon mustard
- 1 teaspoon thyme
- 1 teaspoon Basil shredded
- ½ tsp Seasoned Salt
- 2 tbsp oil
- sugar

- Basil, fresher

PREPARATION

1. Wash and dab the schnitzel and pat it wide with the heel of your hand. Cut the mozzarella into eight thin slices. Season the meat with a little herb salt and the black pepper Brush one side of the schnitzel with mustard, sprinkle with thyme and basil, and top with one slice of ham and two slices of mozzarella per roulade.
2. Heat the oil in a pan and fry the roulades all around for about 10 minutes. Remove the meat rolls and keep them warm (oven at 100 ° C). Cut or dice the garlic cloves, shallots and tomatoes in thin slices and sauté in the frying stock. Add tomato paste, a pinch of sugar and salt each and after a short time deglaze with the warm vegetable stock. Let the whole thing boil down for about 5 - 10 minutes and season with salt and pepper.
3. Arrange the roulades on a plate, pour some sauce over them and garnish with basil leaves. This goes well with rice, pasta and baked potatoes, as well as a fresh green salad.

Preparation time: 35 minutes

Cooking/Baking time: 10 minutes

Serving: 2

INGREDIENTS

- 1 zucchini
- 3 Beefsteak tomato
- 200 g Scampi, frozen
- 200 g Spinach leaves, frozen
- olive oil
- 2 Garlic cloves)
- 3 Red pepper (s)
- 100 g Sheep cheese
- salt
- Pepper, freshly ground
- thyme
- rosemary
- basil
- 100 ml Wine, white

PREPARATION

1. Wash the peppers, tomatoes and zucchini and pat dry.
2. Cut the peppers and tomatoes into small cubes and halve the zucchini and then cut into sheaths. Also cut the sheep's cheese into small cubes. Prepare the spinach leaves according to the instructions on the packet. Then salt the spinach and peel the garlic cloves and add them through the garlic press.
3. Heat the olive oil in a pan and briefly fry the scampi on all sides, remove and set aside.
4. Cook the chopped peppers and the sliced zucchini in the remaining fat until they are firm to the bite. Then add the finely chopped sheep's cheese. Mix everything together and season with the spices and herbs.
5. Grease a baking dish and put the vegetables in there and layer the scampis on top. Pour the white wine over it and let everything au gratin at 200 ° C for 5 minutes.

MEDITERRANEAN ZUCCHINI PAN

Preparation time: 20 minutes
Cooking/Baking time: 20 minutes
Serving: 2

INGREDIENTS

- 1 Onion (s), diced
- 1 Garlic clove (s), pressed
- 4 tbsp olive oil
- 2 Zucchini (approx. 350 g)
- 125 g rice
- 600 ml Vegetable broth
- 100 g Tomato paste
- salt
- pepper
- thyme
- 200 g Feta cheese, diced

PREPARATION

1. Heat the olive oil in a large pan and sweat the onion in it. Wash, quarter and slice the zucchini, add to the onions with the garlic and fry for a while.
2. Add the uncooked rice and fry a little too. Use the whisk to stir the tomato paste into the vegetable stock and use it to deglaze the rice. Then bring everything to a boil. Season to taste with salt, pepper and thyme and simmer for approx. 20 minutes on a low heat until the rice has absorbed the sauce and is cooked through.

3. Stir occasionally (if there is not enough liquid, just stir in a little more vegetable stock). Just before serving, mix the diced feta cheese into the dish and let it flow a little.

MEDITERRANEAN SALMON TROUT

Preparation time: 50 minutes

Cooking/Baking time: 40 minutes

Serving: 3

INGREDIENTS

- 750 g Fish, (salmon trout)
- 5 Garlic cloves)
- 5 Tomato (s), dried
- 1 Lemons)
- 30 ml olive oil
- 10 Olives, black
- 6 small Tomato (s), aromatic
- 200 ml Prosecco or dry white wine
- salt
- Possibly. Herbs

PREPARATION

1. Peel the garlic. Crush two of your toes with a pinch of salt. Squeeze the lemon.
2. Mix the garlic sauce, lemon juice and olive oil with a pinch of salt (if you like, you can replace half of the lemon with 1 tablespoon of balsamic vinegar).
3. Clean the salmon trout, acidify and salt well, also from the inside. Scratch the fish lightly from a distance of about 2 cm. Brush the fish with the olive oil mixture generously (also from the inside). 1 teaspoon should suffice. Allow the trout to marinate in it for 10 minutes.
4. Preheat the oven to 190 ° C top and bottom heat. Heat the roasting pan, add a little olive oil and place the fish on it.
5. Put in the oven and cook there for about 20 minutes. Every 10 Brush with the remaining oil for minutes. (Do not twist the trout, as the fish can fall apart)
6. Meanwhile, halve the tomatoes, dice the dried tomatoes and cut the olives into rings. Add this after 20 minutes with the prosecco and the 3 pressed garlic cloves. Cook for another 5-10 minutes. Then set the oven to the highest setting and grill function for about 5 minutes so that the skin becomes crispy. Serve decorated with lemon wedges.

MEDITERRANEAN VEGETABLE LASAGNA

Preparation time: 30 minutes

Cooking/Baking time: 60 minutes

Serving: 3

INGREDIENTS

- 2 small ones   Onion (noun)
- 750 g   Vegetables (zucchini, peppers, carrots)
- Thyme, fresh, (but it is also possible to dry it)
- 3 tbsp olive oil
- 750 g   Tomato (s), chunky (can)
- salt and pepper
- Lasagne plate (s)
- 150 g   Gouda, grated
- Butter, for the mold

FOR THE BECHAMEL SAUCE:

- 50 g butter
- 2 tbsp flour
- ½ liter milk
- salt and pepper
- nutmeg

PREPARATION

1. Peel the onions and finely dice them. Wash the vegetables and cut them into not too small cubes. Wash fresh thyme and shake dry.
2. Heat olive oil in a saucepan and fry half of the onions in it until translucent. Add the vegetables and sauté briefly. Then fill up with the tomatoes, add the thyme and cook everything over medium heat for 10-15 minutes until al dente. Stir in between. Season well with salt and pepper!
3. Preheat the oven to 200 degrees. To make the bechamel sauce, melt the butter in a saucepan and cook the remaining onions until translucent. Cook for a few minutes after sprinkling with flour. Pour in the milk gradually while stirring. Cook, stirring frequently, for 5 minutes. The sauce should have a slightly thick consistency. Season with nutmeg, salt, and pepper to taste.
4. Grease a baking dish with the butter. Spread some vegetables on the floor. Place the lasagne sheets on top and layer alternately with bechamel sauce, lasagne sheets and vegetables. Finish with béchamel sauce, spread the Gouda on the lasagna and bake the lasagna in the oven on the middle rack at 180 degrees fan-assisted for 40 - 50 minutes until golden brown. Aluminum foil may be required to cover the lasagna. Take out and let stand for approx. 5 minutes before cutting.
5. If you don't like it completely meatless, you can cut 100 g cooked ham into cubes and finally add it to the vegetable mixture.
6. The lasagna can also be prepared very well by preparing the two sauces beforehand and layering everything later.

Preparation time: 20 minutes

Cooking/Baking time: 30 minutes

Serving: 4

INGREDIENTS

- 1 Pumpkin (se)
- 2 Lemon (s), unsprayed
- n. B garlic
- 2 Onion (s), red
- rosemary
- salt and pepper
- thyme
- parsley
- olive oil

PREPARATION

1. Remove the seeds from the pumpkin and cut it into strips. Cut off the peel (not necessary with Hokkaido, but in this case wash the pumpkin well) and place on a baking sheet or in a large baking dish.
2. Cut the onions into narrow strips and the lemons into eighths and add both to the pumpkin. Remove the peel of the garlic cloves (since I like to eat garlic, I already use 5-6 cloves) and add the whole thing too. Season with chopped rosemary, thyme and

parsley, salt and pepper, baste with olive oil and mix everything well. Bake at 180 ° C for about 30 minutes.

LAMB GOULASH THE MEDITERRANEAN WAY

Preparation time: 20 minutes

Cooking/Baking time: 1 hour 45 minutes

Serving: 4

INGREDIENTS

- 600 g Shoulder of lamb
- 250 g Shallot (noun)
- 2 Garlic cloves)
- 1 tbsp, heaped Tomato paste
- 1 large Red pepper (s)
- 3 Tomato (s), fully ripe
- 250 ml Lamb stock or beef stock
- 250 ml Red wine, strong and dry
- 1 bundle Herbs (3 parts thyme, 2 parts rosemary and 1 part bay leaf)
- some Chilli pepper (s), fresh
- salt
- Pepper, black, freshly ground
- 2 tbsp Clarified butter or lard

PREPARATION

1. Peel and cut the onion into eighths, clean and dice the peppers, peel the garlic and chop finely, eighth the tomatoes and cut the meat into not too large pieces. Sear the meat in two portions, season with salt and pepper and keep warm.
2. Then fry the shallot pieces briefly - they should only take on a very light color - add the garlic and briefly roast the tomato paste. Add tomato pieces and deglaze with red wine, reduce briefly, add meat and paprika, fill with stock and add the bouquet of herbs.
3. Simmer in the roaster at 150 ° C with the lid in the oven for about 1.5 hours, take out the pot, remove the bunches, let the goulash boil down for 5 minutes with the lid open and, if necessary, thicken with a little cornstarch dissolved in red wine or cold stock, if a really thick sauce is desired.
4. In addition, small potato spoons from the day before, divided in the middle and seared with garlic and thyme in the pan or just baguette. A fresh bean salad with it is also very tasty.

Preparation time: 20 minutes

Cooking/Baking time: 15 minutes

Serving: 2

INGREDIENTS

- 500 g   Asparagus, green
- 1 tbsp olive oil
- salt and pepper
- 1 Shallot (s), possibly two depending on size
- 10 g butter
- ⅛ liters Vegetable broth
- 100 g   Creme fraiche Cheese
- ½ fret basil
- salt and pepper

FOR THE VINAIGRETTE:

- 1 tbsp Pine nuts
- 2 Tomatoes)
- 1 Shallot (noun)
- 1 teaspoon Lemon juice
- 2 Tea spoons olive oil
- salt and pepper

- sugar

PREPARATION

1. Wash the asparagus, cut off the woody ends. Cook the asparagus stalks in olive oil over medium heat for about 10 minutes while turning. Season with salt and pepper.
2. foam : peel the shallots, dice finely, sauté in butter. Add the vegetable stock, fry the shallots openly until soft, reducing the stock a little. Stir in the crème fraîche. Meanwhile, rinse and dry the basil, then remove the leaves from the stems and cut into strips. Just before serving, put the shallot crème fraîche mixture and basil strips in a blender, puree. Season to taste with salt and pepper.
3. Roast the pine nuts in a pan until golden brown, leave to cool. Quarter the tomatoes, remove the stones, finely dice the pulp. Peel the shallot, also dice finely. Mix the lemon juice with the oil, season with salt, pepper and sugar. Mix in the diced tomatoes and shallots.
4. To serve, pour the tomato vinaigrette over the asparagus and sprinkle with pine nuts. Add a dollop of basil foam and serve the rest separately. Lamb chops and small fried potatoes go well with it.

MEDITERRANEAN PASTA PAN WITH VEGETABLES AND GOAT CHEESE

Preparation time: 25 minutes

Cooking/Baking time: 20 minutes

Serving: 4

INGREDIENTS

- 400 g Pasta (e.g. Spirelli)
- 200 g broccoli
- 1 large Aubergine (noun)
- 1 large zucchini
- 1 large can / n Tomato (s), chopped (800 ml)
- 1 tbsp olive oil
- 3 Garlic cloves)
- 150 g Goat cheese
- 200 g Tomato (s), fresh
- 3 branch / s Rosemary, fresh
- 1 teaspoon, heaped herbs of Provence
- 1 tsp, leveled Thyme, dried
- Chili powder
- n. B Salt and pepper, black from the mill
- 1 tbsp Sour cream

PREPARATION

1. Cook the noodles al dente. Wash broccoli and cut into florets, clean zucchini, cut into pieces, wash eggplant, remove the soft inner part and cut the rest into pieces. Pluck rosemary leaves and finely chop, coarsely crumble goat cheese, cut tomatoes into pieces.
2. Finely chop the garlic and fry in the hot oil. Add broccoli, aubergines and zucchini and fry, season with plenty of salt and pepper. Add chopped tomatoes and let simmer over medium heat for about 10 minutes. Season with salt, pepper, and chili powder and stir in rosemary, Provence herbs, and thyme.
3. When the vegetables are done, turn off the stove and stir in the fresh tomatoes and sour cream. Drain the pasta and add to the vegetables, mix everything together well. Arrange on serving plates and sprinkle with the goat cheese. Serve immediately!

CORDON BLEU CHICKEN WITH MEDITERRANEAN-STYLE POTATOES AND A FRESH SALAD

Preparation time: 45 minutes

Cooking/Baking time: 20 minutes

Serving: 4

INGREDIENTS

- 4th Chicken breasts
- 8 slice / n Butter cheese
- 8 slice / n Ham (Thuringian honey ham)
- 8 tbsp Breadcrumbs
- 2 Egg (s)
- 2 tbsp flour
- 1 tbsp Paprika powder, noble sweet
- 1 tbsp sea-salt
- 10 tbsp peanut oil
- 600 g Potato (s) (triplets)
- 5 tbsp Ketchup (e.g. from Heinz)
- 25 g 8 herbs, TK
- 1 smaller Iceberg lettuce
- 1 smaller Red cabbage
- 3 Carrot

- 1 teaspoon Cayenne pepper
- 30 ml Maple syrup
- 2 tbsp Olive oil, mild

PREPARATION

1. Cut the chicken breasts lengthways into 2 flat escalopes. With a meat mallet, flatten it a little. Season with sea salt and paprika powder.
2. Set up a breading line with a flat plate sprinkled with flour, a slightly taller plate of beaten (whisked) eggs, and a plate of breadcrumbs (which were mixed with a little paprika and sea salt).
3. Fry the schnitzel in hot peanut oil on both sides until golden brown. The temperature should be chosen so that the breading turns golden brown, but the inside is also cooked through.
4. Cover half of the schnitzel with the cheese and half of the ham, then simply fold the other side of the schnitzel onto the topping. Turn the schnitzel wrapped in this manner in the flour, then pull it through the egg mixture before pressing it with the breading.
5. Clean and cut the iceberg lettuce into diamonds. Red cabbage and carrots should be grated into small pieces. Pour into a mixing bowl. Pour the olive oil and maple syrup over the top and thoroughly mix everything together. Season to taste with a little cayenne pepper and refrigerate until ready to eat.
6. For the Mediterranean potatoes, peel the small root nodules and cook in hot water for about 20 minutes. Then pour off the water. Put the ketchup on the potatoes and add the herb mixture as well. Mix everything in well. Arrange everything on plates and serve.

MEDITERRANEAN STYLE BEAN SALAD

Preparation time: 20 minutes

Cooking/Baking time: 10 minutes

Serving: 4

INGREDIENTS

- 750 g   Beans, greens
- salt
- 2 Garlic clove (s), more if desired
- 3 Tomatoes)
- 100 g   Cheese, pecorino (spicy hard cheese made from sheep's milk)
- 4 tbsp olive oil
- 1 tbsp Balsamic vinegar
- 2 Tea spoons mustard
- 2 Tea spoons honey
- pepper
- Thyme, rubbed

PREPARATION

1. Clean the beans first, then cut them into 5 cm pieces. Cook in strong salted water until firm to the bite. In the meantime, peel and finely chop the garlic cloves and dice the tomatoes.

2. Then drain the beans and rinse with cold water until they are just lukewarm. Mix with garlic and tomatoes in a bowl.
3. Grate the pecorino cheese, mix in with the oil, balsamic vinegar, mustard, honey, pepper and thyme. Season to taste after thoroughly mixing everything.
4. Other spicy hard cheeses could be substituted for the pecorino. The salad is great as a side dish for grilling!

Preparation time: 40 minutes

Cooking/Baking time: 25 minutes

Serving: 4

INGREDIENTS

- 4th Chop (s), (stick chop)
- 1 zucchini
- 1 Bell pepper (s), orange
- 1 Tomatoes)
- 2 Garlic cloves)
- 2 tbsp Cream cheese with paprika
- 1 tbsp Paprika pulp
- 1 cup   Gravy
- 1 tbsp Ketchup, (spice ketchup)
- 1 teaspoon salt
- 1 tsp, leveled pepper
- 1 tsp, leveled Paprika powder, hot pink
- 100 g   Mozzarella, grated
- Some water
- ½ cup Sour cream
- 20 g Flakes of butter

PREPARATION

1. Brown the chops on both sides, season with salt and pepper and place in a baking dish. Set the pan aside.
2. Cut the zucchini and peppers into approx. 0.5 cm cubes. Score the tomato, pour boiling water over it, peel and core it and also cut the pulp into cubes.
3. Fry the zucchini and peppers in the pan for about 5 minutes while stirring, squeeze the garlic cloves and fry with them. Then add the paprika pulp and fry as well, add the tomato pieces. Deglaze with a little water and continue to stew. Gradually pour in the meat stock and let it simmer. Then stir in the cream cheese and sour cream and simmer again briefly.
4. Spread the pepper and zucchini mixture over the chops and sprinkle with the grated cheese. Spread a few flakes of butter on top and bake in a preheated oven at 200 degrees with top heat.
5. Boiled potatoes or baguettes and a green salad go well with this. If you want, you can add some Mediterranean herbs, but that's how we like it best. A very fresh dish that can be prepared on the baking sheet for several people.

COLORFUL PAN-FRIED MEDITERRANEAN VEGETABLES WITH RICE

Preparation time: 20 minutes

Cooking/Baking time: 15 minutes

Serving: 2

INGREDIENTS

- 1 m large zucchini
- 5 Tomatoes)
- 3 Bell pepper (s), red, yellow, green
- 400 g Mushrooms
- olive oil
- garlic
- salt and pepper
- 2 bags rice
- 125 g Crème fraîche or sour cream

PREPARATION

1. Cut the vegetables into cubes and quarter the mushrooms. Then put everything in a pan with hot olive oil and steam until the liquid has evaporated. Finally, press in the clove of garlic and season with salt and pepper.
2. At the same time, cook the rice in plenty of salted water. To serve, place everything in a large bowl and mix with the crème fraîche.

MEDITERRANEAN POTATOES FROM THE OVEN

Preparation time: 15 minutes

Cooking/Baking time: 40 minutes

Serving: 4

INGREDIENTS

- 10 m large Waxy potatoes
- 4 branch / s Rosemary, fresh
- 7 sheets Sage, fresh
- 4 toe / n Garlic, with or without peel, cut in half
- n. B Salt, (Fleur de Sel), coarse
- n. B pepper
- Olive oil, for the baking sheet

PREPARATION

1. Rub a roasting pan or baking sheet with oil. Roughly dice the potatoes and add. It is best to only lay one layer so that all potatoes are in contact with the ground. Add the garlic cloves. Salt and pepper well.
2. Drizzle with oil so that as many potatoes as possible get something off. Pluck the needles from the rosemary and add. Add 1-2 twigs as a whole. Place the sage leaves between the potatoes.
3. Bake the whole thing in the hot oven for about 30-40 minutes at 200 degrees, until all the potatoes are crispy all around and have a brown color.

4. Goes well with grilled food or just with salad. Accompanied by a glass of red wine from Tuscany or Piedmont.

MEDITERRANEAN CHICKEN AND VEGETABLE PAN

Preparation time: 30 minutes

Cooking/Baking time: 25 minutes

Serving: 3

INGREDIENTS

- 3 Chicken breast fillet (s)
- n. B soy sauce
- 1 large Onion (noun)
- 1 Red pepper (s)
- 1 m large zucchini
- 1 Aubergine (noun)
- 2 Tomato (s), or 1 handful of cherry tomatoes
- 3 toe / n garlic
- 1 Chilli pepper (s), red
- 3 tbsp Tomato paste
- 50 ml cream
- 2 tbsp Pesto (wild garlic)
- 3 tbsp Cream cheese, for example with chilli
- thyme
- salt and pepper
- sugar
- Cardamom powder

- Cinnamon powder
- olive oil
- Lemon juice

PREPARATION

1. Cut the fillets into bite-sized cubes and marinate in 4-5 tablespoons soy sauce.
2. Cut the onion into half rings. Roughly dice the paprika and zucchini. Cut the aubergine into slices, season with salt, dab off after about 10 minutes and chop coarsely. Cut the garlic into slices, the chilli pepper into small cubes and the tomato into large pieces.
3. Heat the olive oil in a large pan, sear the meat in it, add the onions and thyme and braise briefly. Remove both, and now add the vegetables (except the tomatoes) to the pan, fry them, deglaze with about 1/4 l water, add spices, pesto, and tomato paste, and cook for about 10 minutes with the lid closed.
4. Then add the tomatoes, cream, cream cheese and the meat with the onions, mix everything well and simmer for another 5 minutes over low heat. Season to taste with salt and pepper. If you like, you can add a few squirts of lemon juice. That gives a fine, fresh note.

Preparation time: 15 minutes
Cooking/Baking time: 5 minutes
Serving: 2

INGREDIENTS

- 2 Chicory
- 4 tbsp olive oil
- 4 cl Balsamic, red or white
- 4 small ones Tomatoes)
- 1 tbsp herbs of Provence
- Some salt
- some Pepper, black, freshly ground

PREPARATION

1. A (large) pan with a lid is required. Remove the outer leaves of the chicory and cut into lengthways slices as thick as a finger.
2. Heat the oil in a pan, fry the chicory slices on both sides. Deglaze with the balsamic vinegar and immediately put the pan lid on top. Let simmer until the chicory is firm to the bite (do not let it get too soft).
3. Then halve the tomatoes (possibly eighth for larger tomatoes) and add to the chicory - just let them heat up (they shouldn't get mushy!).
4. Salt and pepper the vegetables and pour the Provence herbs over them. Mix. Arrange nicely on plates. Baguette can be served with it.

Preparation time: 20 minutes

Cooking/Baking time: 30 minutes

Serving: 4

INGREDIENTS

- 1 kg Potato (s), quartered, with skin
- 1 thick Zucchini, sliced
- 1 large Pepper (s), color of your choice, cut into strips
- 1 large Onion (s), quartered
- 500 g Mushrooms, fresh, in large slices
- some stems Rosemary, sage, thyme, oregano
- salt and pepper
- Garlic clove (s), amount to taste
- olive oil

PREPARATION

1. Place the vegetables, mushrooms and potatoes in an ovenproof pan. Sprinkle the chopped herbs, if possible fresh, and the chopped garlic on top. Salt and pepper and pour a good portion of olive oil over everything.

2. Mix together and bake in the oven at 200 degrees for about 30 minutes, turning once or twice. When the potatoes are done, they can be served.

MEDITERRANEAN CHICKEN BREAST FROM THE OVEN

Preparation time: 10 minutes

Cooking/Baking time: 20 minutes

Serving: 2

INGREDIENTS

- 2 Chicken breast fillet (s)
- 1 ½ tbsp Olive paste, (tapenade), black
- 2 Tomatoes)
- n. B salt and pepper
- 1 ball Mozzarella
- 1 teaspoon Oregano, dried
- n. B Paprika powder

PREPARATION

1. Divide the chicken breast into two flat cutlets. Spread the schnitzel on both sides with the tapenade. Season with salt and pepper. Place in a baking dish.
2. Top the chicken breast with tomatoes and mozzarella. Season with oregano, salt, pepper, and paprika to taste.
3. Bake for 15-20 minutes at 220 ° C in the center of the oven. Rice pairs well with this, and gnocci are also suggested as a side dish.

MEDITERRANEAN POLLO FINO WITH CRISPY ROSEMARY AND POTATO WEDGES

Preparation time: 30 minutes

Cooking/Baking time: 45 minutes

Serving: 3

INGREDIENTS

- 6th Chicken legs, boned (Pollo Fino)
- 2 tbsp olive oil
- 1 tbsp Balsamic bianco
- 1 tsp, leveled Mustard medium hot
- 1 tsp, leveled honey
- 1 Garlic cloves)
- 4 branch / s thyme
- 2 branch / s rosemary
- 2 sheets sage
- ½ fret chives
- ¼ bunch parsley
- ¼ bunch dill
- 1 tsp, leveled salt
- ¼ tsp, worked   Paprika powder, noble sweet

- ¼ tsp, worked   pepper
- For the baked potatoes: (rosemary and potato wedges)
- 600 g Potato (s), small (e.g. gourmet potatoes or triplets)
- 300 ml Salt water
- 3 Bay leaves
- 4 branch / s   rosemary
- 2 tbsp olive oil
- 2 Garlic cloves)
- ½ tsp, worked   Paprika powder, noble sweet
- 1 teaspoon   salt
- ¼ tsp, worked   pepper
- ¼ tsp, worked   Caraway seeds, possibly

PREPARATION

1. Marinade the boned chicken thighs and the potato wedges about 4 hours beforehand. Chop all herbs and garlic cloves as finely as possible and season with olive oil, balsamic vinegar, mustard, honey, salt, paprika and pepper. Mix together with the boned chicken thighs in a freezer bag and leave to steep in the refrigerator for about 3 hours. Important: it is essential to use fresh herbs for a full herbal taste!

2. For the rosemary potato wedges, pre-cook the gourmet potatoes (are very small potatoes with a fine skin) whole (with skin) in boiling salted water with bay leaves for approx. 5 - max. 10 minutes (depending on the size of the potatoes). Then let cool a little, then divide or quarter.

3. Chop the rosemary and garlic cloves very finely, mix with olive oil, paprika, salt and pepper (if you like: also with caraway seeds) and mix carefully with the potatoes in a mixing bowl. Let it soak in the refrigerator for about 3 hours.

4. After the chicken legs and potatoes have been pulled through nicely, preheat the oven to 180 ° C (convection).

5. Take the chicken legs out of the marinade and remove some of the herbs (they would only burn later). Filter the remaining marinade through a sieve and place the filtered herbs on the bottom of a smaller baking dish.

6. Fry the cleaned Pollo Fino briefly in a hot pan on the skin side until the skin is lightly tanned. Then place them close together, with the skin side up, in the baking dish on the bed of herbs.

7. Bake for about 40 - 45 minutes until crispy. Brush the skin side 2-3 times with light salt water in the first 20 minutes.

8. Bake the potato wedges with the marinade in another baking dish together with the chicken legs until crispy brown. A light tomato and mozzarella salad and a cool white wine go well with it.

Preparation time: 15 minutes
Cooking/Baking time: 15 minutes
Serving: 2

INGREDIENTS

- 125 g Ebly, nature
- 1 tbsp olive oil
- 1 Onion (noun)
- 1 Red pepper (s)
- 1 Bell pepper (s), green
- 1 m-tall zucchini
- 2 Tea spoons Rosemary, fresh, finely chopped
- 1 large Garlic clove (s), finely chopped
- 4 tsp Pesto rosso, from the glass
- 75 g Cheese, small cubes (Gouda, Gryere or Feta)

PREPARATION

1. Bring salted water to the boil and let the Ebly simmer uncovered for 10 minutes. Pour into a colander and drain thoroughly. Cut the peppers and zucchino into 15 mm cubes and the onion into narrow wedges.
2. Heat the oil, first fry the onion wedges briefly, then add the paprika, zucchini and rosemary and fry vigorously. Reduce the heat, add the garlic and cook everything al dente for 3-4 minutes. Add the Ebly, mix in the pesto and turn the heat down to very low.

3. Spread the cheese cubes on the mass and close the pan with a lid. After 2-3 minutes the cheese will melt.

WHAT IS A VEGAN DIET?

Following a vegan diet is appropriate for everyone. The veganism is a way of life that tries to prevent all forms of exploitation and cruelty to animals, including the use of animals for food, clothing and footwear, cosmetics and any other activity that causes death or suffering such as circuses, zoos, and horse races.

Veganism opposes the use of animals in medical and military research and advocates for the development of safer, more efficient, and humane alternatives. Vegan diet regarding food, the vegan person follows a 100% vegetable diet, that is, a diet in which all types of meat, fish and shellfish, dairy products, eggs and honey are excluded. Although for most of the people who live in Western countries and who base their diet on animal products, this sounds restrictive, the truth is that a 100% plant-based diet can and in fact tends to be much more varied than the typical Western diet . This is so because vegan people include many plant foods in their diet that, having been part of the traditional diet for centuries has recently been relegated in favor of animal foods.

WHAT THE VEGAN DIET INCLUDES, IN ADDITION TO ALL KINDS OF FRUITS AND VEGETABLES, IS:

Whole grains

Not just bread, rice and pasta. Other cereals and pseudo-cereals such as oats, corn, millet, amaranth, quinoa or barley are a regular part of the vegan diet. Seitan is obtained from wheat gluten, a vegetable "meat" rich in protein and minerals that has been part of the Asian diet for centuries.

Vegetables

In addition to chickpeas, beans, lentils and peas, vegan diets include soy and its derivatives (tofu, tempeh, miso, and milk and soy yogurt), foods rich in protein, minerals and vitamins and with a much healthier fat profile than products of animal origin. Peanuts also belong to the legume family and far from being a mere appetizer or snack, they are part of traditional Asian cuisine, as well as being the base of the famous peanut butter, with which you can prepare sandwiches, smoothies and many desserts.

Nuts and seeds

Walnuts, almonds, hazelnuts, cashews, pine nuts, macadamia nuts, Brazil nuts, pumpkin and sunflower seeds, sesame, flax, chia ... foods that are forgotten in today's diet and yet are nutritionally and culinary very interesting, as well as have very beneficial effects on health.

Mushrooms

All kinds of edible mushrooms and mushrooms are usually included in a vegan diet, providing flavor and nutrients to rice dishes, pasta, soups, salads and empanadas.

Algae

Seaweed is the vegetable of the sea and has been part of the culinary traditions of many coastal peoples, such as the Japanese, the Irish or the Galicians. Although it is difficult to find them in conventional restaurants, seaweed has its special place in the kitchen of vegans due to its characteristic flavor and its nutritional properties.

WHO CAN FOLLOW A VEGAN DIET?

This was recognized once again by the American Academy of Nutrition at the end of last year. A balanced and well-planned vegan diet "is suitable for all stages of life, including pregnancy, lactation, childhood, adolescence, adulthood and old age, as well as for athletes."

WHY CHOOSE A VEGAN DIET?

It is becoming increasingly clear that animal consumption is the main cause of many of the world's problems. Since plant-based nutrition is a concrete solution to these issues, a lifestyle and a diet without animal products are rapidly gaining momentum. A plant-based diet saves animals from suffering, reduces individual ecological footprints, and helps to create a more just world. At the same time, eating a plant-based diet can also contribute to a more varied and healthy diet.

WHAT TO EAT IF YOU FOLLOW A VEGAN DIET

A diet without animal products is extremely versatile. The transition to a more plant-based diet opens up a world of exciting new culinary possibilities. Products of animal origin can be easily substituted. The fruits and vegetables such as tomatoes, cabbage, squash, garlic, olives, broccoli, apples, and nectarines, fruits of the forest, bananas, melons and oranges are foods that are important source vitamins, minerals, phytonutrients and fiber. The pulses such as lentils, peas, beans, soybeans and lupins are an important source of protein.

The whole grains and cereals such as oats, rye, spelled, wheat, barley, millet and rice, along with pseudocereals like quinoa, amaranth and buckwheat, contribute complex carbohydrates, fiber and phytochemicals.

The nuts and seeds like flax seeds, walnuts and hemp seeds provide healthy fats and nutrients with high nutritional value. The vegan meat alternatives such as tofu, vegan burgers, sausages escalope and can be found in many versions made, for example, soybeans, wheat gluten and lupine. There are also vegan alternatives for milk, yogurt, and cheese. These are normally made with soybeans, nuts and cereals. The vegan plate offers a simple guide on how to choose healthy foods. The composition of the plate matches current scientific knowledge about the effects of the food and beverages we take on our health.

WHAT TO AVOID ON A VEGAN DIET

❖ Vegans avoid the consumption of animal meat, derived from animal products and foods that contain ingredients of animal origin. This includes the following:
❖ Red meat and poultry from animals such as cows, pigs, horses, chicken and turkeys.
❖ Fish and other marine animals such as all species of fish, squid, mussels, crabs and lobsters.
❖ Dairy like milk, cheese, yogurt, and butter.
❖ Eggs such as chicken eggs and caviar.
❖ Honey and other bee products.
❖ Ingredients of animal origin such as gelatin, lactose, whey, shellac, carmine and omega 3 fatty acids derived from fish.

A VEGAN DIET THAT IS WELL-BALANCED IS A HEALTHY DIET.

High consumption of animal products is one of the leading causes of the most common lifestyle-related diseases such as obesity, diabetes, and cardiovascular disease. A varied and balanced plant diet can help reduce the risk of developing these diseases. In a report on these issues, the Academy of Nutrition and Dietetics states that a well-planned vegan (as well as vegetarian) diet is appropriate at any stage of life, be it during pregnancy, infancy, childhood, and adolescence. 1

In addition, a plant-based diet reduces the risk of food poisoning caused by salmonella and other bacteria and exposure to environmental toxins.

VEGAN RECIPES

Preparation time: 30 minutes

Cooking/Baking time: 45 minutes

Serving: 1

INGREDIENTS

FOR THE DOUGH:

- 330 g Whole wheat flour
- 150 g Margarine, vegan
- 80 ml water
- ½ tsp sea-salt

FOR THE FILLING:

- 400 g Cherry tomato
- 400 g Silken tofu
- 2 tbsp olive oil
- 2 tbsp food starch
- 1 teaspoon sea-salt
- 1 teaspoon turmeric
- 1 pinch (s) Nutmeg, freshly grated

- some   Pepper, freshly ground
- 1 teaspoon Thyme, fresh
- 1 teaspoon Oregano, fresh
- 1 tbsp Chives, fresh
- 3 tbsp Basil, fresh

PREPARATION

1. For the quiche dough, process all the dough ingredients into a smooth dough and cover for 30 minutes in the refrigerator.
2. Wash and dry the tomatoes before cutting them in half for the filling. To make a creamy mass, puree the silken tofu with the oil, cornstarch, salt, and spices. Wash and dry the fresh herbs before chopping them finely and stirring them into the filling.
3. Roll out the dough to the size of a quiche tin plus the rim on a large piece of baking paper and slide it into the quiche tin with the baking paper. Press the dough firmly against the mold, as well as the edge.
4. Pre-bake in a hot oven at 200 ° C top / bottom heat for 10 minutes. Then distribute the filling on the dough and cover the filling with the halved tomatoes with the skin side down (so the water in the tomatoes does not soften the quiche).
5. Bake the quiche in the hot oven for another 20 minutes. Then reduce the temperature to 175 ° C and bake the quiche for another 15 minutes. Let the quiche rest for 10 minutes before cutting and then serve.

ORIENTAL STUFFED TOMATOES

Preparation time: 20 minutes

Cooking/Baking time: 25 minutes

Serving: 3

INGREDIENTS

- 200 g couscous
- 50 g Raisins
- salt
- 50 g Pine nuts
- 1 teaspoon Coriander seeds
- 2 stems mint
- 6 large Tomato (s) approx. 170 - 220 g
- 2 Tea spoons Cinnamon powder
- 1 Garlic cloves)
- 2 tbsp olive oil
- 2 Tea spoons Curry powder, spicy, e.g. B. Madras curry
- Oil for the mold

PREPARATION

1. Preheat the oven to 200 ° C top / bottom heat. Pour double the amount of boiling salted water over the couscous and raisins and let it steep according to the instructions on the packet.
2. Roast the pine nuts in a pan, turning frequently, until they begin to smell. Allow to cool on a plate immediately. Wash the tomatoes, remove the stem, and cut off the lid. With a spoon, hollow out the inside, remove the watery seeds, and finely cut the pulp and lid.
3. Place the coriander seeds in a mortar and crush them finely. Wash and dry the mint, then pluck and finely chop the leaves. Peel the garlic and mash it with a press.
4. Fluff the couscous with two forks and mix with all the prepared ingredients. Pour the mixture into the tomatoes.
5. Grease a baking dish thinly with oil. Place the tomatoes side by side in the tin. Bake in the hot oven for about 15-20 minutes.

PUMPKIN CREAM SOUP

Preparation time: 20 minutes

Cooking/Baking time: 30 minutes

Serving: 6

INGREDIENTS

- 2 Hokkaido pumpkin (se)
- 800 g   Carrot
- 2 m.-large Potatoes)
- ¼ tuber / n celery
- 1 piece (s) Ginger, approx. 7 cm
- 2 small ones   Chilli pepper
- 1 Garlic cloves)
- 1 m.-large Onion (noun)
- 1.2 liters Vegetable broth
- 1 can   Coconut milk
- 1 teaspoon Curry powder
- salt and pepper
- nutmeg
- oil

PREPARATION

1. Peel the carrots, potatoes, ginger, onions, celery, and garlic, and core the pumpkin and chili peppers. Everything should be cut into cubes and fried briefly in a little oil in a large saucepan. Sprinkle with curry powder and deglaze with stock. Simmer for about 30 minutes on a low heat.
2. When all of the vegetables have softened, puree the soup in a blender. If it's too thick, thin it out with a little more vegetable stock. Season with salt and pepper, then stir in the coconut milk. Return to the heat and stir with the blender before serving.

VEGAN FLAMBÉE TART WITH SMOKED TOFU AND CASHEW BUTTER

Preparation time: 10 minutes

Cooking/Baking time: 20 minutes

Serving: 1

INGREDIENTS

FOR THE DOUGH:

- 250 g flour
- 125 ml water
- 2 tbsp olive oil
- 1 pinch (s)   alt
- Flour for the work surface

FOR COVERING:

- 100 g Cashew butter, organic
- 65 ml water
- 2 Tea spoons Lemon juice, freshly squeezed
- 1 pinch (s) nutmeg
- 2 large Onion (s), red
- 100 g Smoked tofu
- 2 tbsp olive oil

- n. B Salt and pepper, freshly ground
- ½ fret chives

PREPARATION

1. Preheat the oven to 210 ° C on top and bottom heat. Knead the dough ingredients together to form a homogeneous dough. Form the dough into a ball and set it aside for a minute.
2. Cut the smoked tofu into fine cubes. Heat the olive oil in a pan and fry the tofu cubes on all sides for about 3 minutes. Set the pan aside.
3. Mix the cashew butter with lemon juice and water until creamy and season with salt, pepper and nutmeg. Peel the onions and cut into fine rings.
4. Roll out the dough thinly on a lightly floured work surface to the size of a baking sheet and place on a baking sheet lined with baking paper. Brush with cashew cream, then top with onion rings and evenly distribute the smoked tofu.
5. Bake the tarte flambée in the hot oven on the middle rack for about 15-20 minutes. Finally, wash the chives, shake dry, cut into small pieces and sprinkle the finished tarte flambée with them.

Preparation time: 15 minutes
Cooking/Baking time: 15 minutes
Serving: 2

INGREDIENTS

- 2 Paprika (s), colorful
- 1 toe / n garlic
- 1 can Coconut milk
- 4th Mushrooms
- some olive oil
- 2 Tea spoons herbs of Provence
- 3 tsp Curry powder
- 3 tbsp Tomato paste
- salt and pepper
- Paprika powder
- Cinnamon powder

PREPARATION

1. First dice the paprika, mushrooms and the clove of garlic, fry in a little olive oil and add Provence herbs.
2. Now deglaze with the coconut milk, stir well, add a little water depending on the consistency of the milk and bring to the boil. Then let it simmer a little while seasoning with salt, pepper, paprika powder, a little cinnamon and curry powder.

Finally mix in the tomato paste. Cook to the desired consistency and season again before serving.

MEDITERRANEAN TOFU STEW

Preparation time: 20 minutes
Cooking/Baking time: 30 minutes
Serving: 4

INGREDIENTS

- 180 g Tofu mince
- 1 large Onion (noun)
- 1 toe / n garlic
- 1 large zucchini
- 1 small Aubergine (noun)
- 250 g Mushrooms
- 1 tbsp Tomato paste
- 1 can Tomatoes, chunky
- 150 ml Vegetable broth
- 1 tbsp oil
- Some salt and pepper
- Some Herbs, Italian

PREPARATION

1. Finely dice the onion and sauté in a little oil. Then add the tofu mince and fry. Finely chop the garlic and add to the tofu together with the tomato paste. Deglaze with vegetable stock.
2. Cut the aubergine and zucchini into 0.5 cm cubes and add to the tofu with the tomatoes; simmer for about 10 minutes. Cook for another 10 minutes after adding the mushrooms in slices and the Italian herbs. Season with salt and pepper to taste

SWEET POTATO CURRY WITH COCONUT AND PEANUT SAUCE

Preparation time: 60 minutes

Cooking/Baking time: 60 minutes

Serving: 12

INGREDIENTS

- 3 kg Sweet potato
- 8th Onion (noun)
- 4th Carrot
- 4 cm Ginger root
- 1 liter Coconut milk
- 200 g Peanuts, salted
- 4 tbsp Curry powder
- 3 tbsp Broth, grains
- 1 tube / n Tomato paste
- 4 toe / n garlic
- 1 small Glass Sambal Oelek
- 1 bunch Coriander green
- n. B salt
- some Oil, for frying

PREPARATION

1. Peel the onions and finely dice them. Press the garlic. Finely chop the ginger and peanuts. Peel the carrots and sweet potatoes and cut into 1 cm cubes.
2. Roast the sweet potatoes and carrots in hot oil in a large roasting pan and set aside. Then fry the onions in a pan in hot oil, add the garlic, curry and ginger. Finally add tomato paste, granulated stock, sambal oelek and peanuts and roast briefly. Add coconut milk and reduce a little. Then, season the mixture with salt and pour it over the sweet potatoes in the roaster.
3. Braise in a preheated oven at 175 ° C without a lid for about 60 minutes. Stir again and again. Sprinkle with chopped coriander before serving. Basmati rice goes well with it.

Preparation time: 25 minutes

Cooking/Baking time: 30 minutes

Serving: 4

INGREDIENTS

- 1 piece (s) Celeriac, about 1/5 tuber
- 2 Carrot
- 2 Onion (noun)
- olive oil
- 150 g Soy shredded meat, fine
- 1 pck. Tomatoes, strained, approx. 500 g
- ½ tube / n Tomato paste
- salt and pepper
- Paprika powder, noble sweet
- Curry powder
- 500 g Whole wheat spaghetti or spirelli
- Soy milk (soy drink) or soy cream, to taste

PREPARATION

1. Put the soy strips in a bowl and pour boiling water over them according to the instructions on the packet, stir and set aside. Peel and finely chop the carrots, onions, and celery.
2. In a pan, heat the olive oil, then add the vegetables and cook for 5 - 7 minutes on a low heat with the lid closed.
3. Strain the soy slices and add them to the pan with the rest of the ingredients. Fry without the lid until crispy. This may take some time because the soy meat has a lot of water stored. Searing may necessitate a little more oil as well.
4. When the soy slices are well seared (now is also a good time to put the noodles on), add the tomato paste to the pan and mix with the soy and vegetable mix. Also add the tomatoes and keep stirring. Season to taste with the spices and salt.
5. The Bolognese is now ready and can be served with the cooked pasta.

PASTA IN A PHONY MUSHROOM CREAM SAUCE TOPPED WITH ROCKET

Preparation time: 15 minutes
Cooking/Baking time: 10 minutes
Serving: 2

INGREDIENTS

- 250 g pasta
- 1 bunch arugula
- 250 g Mushrooms
- 50 g Cashew nuts, unsalted
- 2 tbsp Yeast flakes
- 2 tbsp Rice Cream (Rice Cream Cuisine)
- 1 toe / n garlic
- 1 teaspoon mustard
- Some nutmeg
- salt and pepper
- Vegetable broth, instant
- water

PREPARATION

1. Cook the pasta until al dente in salted water, then drain. The rocket should be cleaned and roughly chopped. Clean the mushrooms and cook them until the liquid has evaporated in a pan. Remove the pan from the heat.

2. In a blender, combine the cashew nuts, yeast flakes, rice cream, mustard, garlic, and nutmeg. Stir in the water gradually until the sauce reaches the desired consistency. Season with salt, freshly ground pepper, and some grained vegetable stock to taste.

3. Mix in the sauce with the mushrooms and pasta. Arrange on plates and spread the rocket on top.

Preparation time: 40 minutes

Cooking/Baking time: 25 minutes

Serving: 4

INGREDIENTS

- 900 g Potato (s), waxy potatoes
- 4th Onion (noun)
- 2 tbsp flour
- 6 tbsp Margarine, vegan (e.g. Alsan)
- 250 ml Soy cream (soy cream cuisine) or normal sweet cream (but then it is not vegan)
- 400 ml Vegetable broth, depending on the consistency, more
- 400 g Chanterelles, thawed or fresh
- 2 federal government Herbs, at will
- 1 bunch chives
- Some salt and pepper
- Some nutmeg

PREPARATION

1. For the bechamel potatoes, peel and finely dice 2 onions, peel the potatoes and cut into 1 cm cubes. Heat 2 tablespoons of margarine in a pan and fry the onions and potatoes all around.
2. For the bechamel sauce, melt 2 tablespoons of margarine in a saucepan and stir in the flour with a whisk. Deglaze with the vegetable stock and beat vigorously. Mix in the cream and nutmeg. Now add the bechamel sauce to the potatoes and cook them for about 8 minutes. Possibly add stock. Season with salt and pepper to taste.
3. Finely chop the herbs for the herb chanterelles. The remaining onions should be finely diced. Brown the onions in a pan with 2 tablespoons margarine. Fry the chanterelles all over, whether they are thawed or fresh. Stir in the herbs and cook for 3 minutes. Season with salt and pepper.
4. Arrange the bechamel potatoes and chanterelles on plates and garnish with chopped chives.

Preparation time: 45 minutes

Cooking/Baking time: 4 hour

Serving: 8

INGREDIENTS

FOR THE SAUCE: (VEGAN BOLOGNESE)

- 250 g Tofu, natural
- 250 g Smoked tofu
- 2 m large Onion (noun)
- 300 g Mushrooms
- 2 large Carrot
- 5 rod / n Celery
- 4 toe / n garlic
- 1 Hot peppers
- 4 tbsp soy sauce
- 1 tbsp Raw cane sugar
- 75 g Tomato paste
- 1 teaspoon Paprika powder, hot pink
- 200 ml White wine, dry
- 2 liters water

- 1 tbsp Vegetable broth (powder)
- 2 Tea spoons Thyme, dried
- 2 Bay leaves
- Nutmeg, freshly grated
- 1 teaspoon sea-salt
- Black pepper from the mill
- 2 pot basil
- 5 tbsp Rapeseed oil for frying, mild
- 500 g Spinach leaves, optional

FOR THE BECHAMEL SAUCE:

- 75 g Margarine, vegan
- 75 g wheat flour
- 1 liter Soy drink (soy drink calcium), cold
- 250 ml Soy Cream (Soy Cream Cuisine) (Soy Cuisine)
- ½ Lemon (s), the juice of it
- Nutmeg, freshly grated
- 1 teaspoon sea-salt
- Black pepper from the mill

ASIDE FROM THAT:

- 1 pck Lasagne plate (s)
- 300 g Cheese, vegan (Wilmersburger organic pizza melt strong)
- 1 tbsp Margarine for greasing the mold, vegan

PREPARATION

1. It was a success after several attempts: the recipe for the perfect vegan lasagna, according to me and the opinions of various test eaters!
2. To make the Bolognese, crumble the tofu into a chop-like, crumbly consistency. This can be done with a fork, but it is preferable to do with your hands. Peel the onions and garlic, dice the onions and mushrooms, finely grate the carrots and celery, and chop the garlic and peppers.
3. Heat 4 tablespoons of rapeseed oil in a large roasting pan and first fry only the tofu mince over high heat until it is evenly brown (not just "browned"). Compared to searing traditional minced meat, this requires a significantly higher level of patience and fat. If necessary, add more oil during the roasting process and do not show any false shyness; after all, the fat content of "normal" minced meat is approx. 30%, whereas that of tofu is only approx. 9%.
4. When the tofu is brown, add the onion cubes and let them take on color. Take the fried tofu and onion mixture out of the roaster and set aside.
5. Sear the diced mushrooms in a tablespoon of rapeseed oil and let them brown, then add the carrots and celery and fry. Add the garlic, chili peppers, soy sauce and the tofu and onion mixture and simmer everything together for a few more minutes.

6. Then, make a space in the center and place the tablespoons of raw cane sugar directly on the bottom of the roaster to caramelize. Combine the tomato paste and paprika powder with the caramelized sugar and sauté for a few minutes. Then, thoroughly combine the contents of the roast, season with salt and freshly ground pepper, and deglaze with the white wine. After the white wine has boiled off completely, pour in the water and stir in the vegetable stock powder and the two teaspoons of thyme. Finally add some freshly ground nutmeg and the two bay leaves.

7. The Bolognese must now be simmered gently for at least 3 hours, stirring occasionally without the lid; it is ready after about 5 hours. The long cooking time is really an important part of this recipe.

8. If necessary, add a little more water during the cooking process, but keep in mind that the finished sauce should have a thick, ragout-like consistency at the end.

9. When the cooking time is up, remove the bay leaves. Finely chop the basil and stir it into the finished sauce. Finally season with salt and pepper.

10. For the béchamel sauce, melt the vegan margarine in a saucepan and let it get hot. Dust with the flour and sauté briefly. Then pour the cold Soy milk into the pot, stirring constantly with a whisk, and then add the soy cuisine. Let the sauce simmer for about 10 minutes so that it bonds nicely and the flour taste evaporates. Make sure to keep stirring, otherwise the sauce will start immediately!

11. Add the lemon juice and season with salt, pepper and freshly grated nutmeg. Grease a large lasagne dish with vegan margarine. First cover the bottom of the pan with a thin layer of Bolognese. Place a layer of lasagne sheets on top. Pour a layer of Bolognese over the pasta, followed by a layer of bechamel. Repeat this process in the order shown (pasta, Bolognese, Béchamel) until the sauces are used up. Depending on how juicy you want your lasagna to be, the ratio of pasta to sauce can be varied at this point.

12. Before the top and last layer is applied, mix the pizza melt with the remaining béchamel sauce to a thick paste. This is critical in order for the vegan cheese to melt authentically and evenly when gratinated. The béchamel and cheese mixture therefore forms the top and final layer of the lasagna. Spread it evenly with the help of a tablespoon.

13. Bake in the oven preheated to 200 ° C for about 40 - 45 minutes until the cheese has a golden brown crust.

14. The lasagna is also very tasty, although a little less classic, if you add spinach to the Bolognese. To do this, put approx. 500 g of spinach leaves in a saucepan with a little water and wait until the spinach has collapsed. Then rinse with cold water, drain and chop. The spinach can be added after the Bolognese has been deglazed. The lasagna is best served with a glass of dry red wine and a few close friends.

VEGAN TURKISH PIZZA - SEBZELI LAHMACUN

Preparation time: 45 minutes

Cooking/Baking time: 30 minutes

Serving: 8

INGREDIENTS

FOR THE FILLING: VARIANT 1

- 2 rod / n leek
- 1 large Onion (noun)
- 3 Tomatoes)
- Olive oil for frying
- 1 teaspoon salt
- 1 teaspoon pepper
- 1 teaspoon Pul beaver
- 1 teaspoon Peppermint, dried
- 50 ml water

FOR THE FILLING: VARIANT 2

- 1 Red pepper (s)
- 1 large Onion (noun)

- Oil for frying
- 1 tbsp Paprika pulp
- ½ tbsp Tomato paste
- ½ tbsp thyme
- ½ tbsp Peppermint, dried
- 1 teaspoon cumin
- 2 Tea spoons Pul beaver
- 1 bowl Walnuts
- 2 tbsp sesame

FOR THE DOUGH:

- 1 kg flour
- 1 pck Fresh yeast
- 1 tbsp salt
- 650 ml Water, lukewarm

PREPARATION

1. Wash and chop the leek, chop the onion, and peel and chop the tomatoes for the first filling. Fry the onion in olive oil, add the tomatoes and fry with them. Then add the leek and fry until it becomes soft. After the leek has softened, season with the spices and add 50 ml of water. Simmer until the liquid has evaporated.
2. For the second filling, cut the bell pepper and onion into small pieces and fry in oil. Turn off the heat after adding the paprika and tomato paste. Now stir in the spices. Then finely chop the walnuts and add the sesame seeds to the filling, mix well, and set aside to cool.
3. To make the dough, combine all of the ingredients, knead into a dough, and let rise in a warm place for 30 minutes. Preheat the oven to 200°C top/bottom heat.
4. Make small balls out of the dough. With a rolling pin, roll out the balls to the size of a cake plate and spread the filling over them.
5. Exactly four pieces fit on one sheet. Bake in the hot oven on the lowest setting for about four to five minutes. While the first four are baking, prepare the next four and then bake. Continue until the batter and fillings are used up.

VEGETABLE STIR-FRY THAI STYLE WITH WHITE ASPARAGUS

Preparation time: 30 minutes

Cooking/Baking time: 20 minutes

Serving: 4

INGREDIENTS

- 500 g   Asparagus, white
- 2 Onion (noun)
- 250 g   Mushrooms
- 2 m large Red pepper (s)
- 1 piece (s) Ginger root, approx. 5 cm
- 2 Garlic cloves)
- 1 stick / n Lemongrass
- Little Oil for frying
- Teriyaki sauce
- soy sauce
- 1 glass Mung bean seedlings, possibly fresh ones
- 1 glass Bamboo shoot
- 200 ml Coconut milk
- n. B Chili powder

PREPARATION

1. Peel the asparagus and clean the other vegetables. Cut the onions into half-rings, and the asparagus, bell pepper, and mushrooms into bite-size pieces. Chop the ginger and garlic finely, and cut the lemongrass into large pieces (so that you can fish it out later).
2. In a pan or wok, heat a little vegetable oil and sear the cut vegetables in it. If using fresh sprouts, add them at the end. Fry the garlic, ginger, lemongrass, and other spices in hot oil.
3. Turn the temperature down a little and now deglaze with teriyaki sauce and soy sauce, depending on how salty or sweet you like it. Then add the drained sprouts and the jar's bamboo. Return to the boil for a few seconds after adding the coconut milk. The vegetables should have a firm bite to them.
4. Instead of fresh ginger and lemongrass, try a heaping teaspoon of powder and, of course, fresh chili peppers instead of chili powder. Non-vegetarians can add a few dashes of fish sauce in addition to soy and teriyaki sauce. Stir-fried vegetables go well with basmati rice or another fragrant rice.

VEGAN LEMON AND FENNEL RISOTTO

Preparation time: 10 minutes

Cooking/Baking time: 25 minutes

Serving: 4

INGREDIENTS

- 1 Onion (noun)
- 1 large Fennel bulb
- 2 tbsp olive oil
- 200 g Risotto rice
- 150 ml White wine, vegan
- 1 Garlic cloves)
- 0.7 liters Vegetable broth
- 2 tbsp Capers
- 1 teaspoon, heaped Almond butter, white
- 1 tbsp Yeast flakes
- 1 Organic lemon (s), grated zest and juice from them
- 1 handful basil
- salt and pepper

PREPARATION

1. Cut the onion and fennel into small cubes. Keep the fennel green for later. Fry the onions and fennel together in the olive oil. Add the risotto rice until it is translucent. Deglaze with the white wine and let the wine boil down.
2. Add the pressed or very finely chopped garlic. Pour in the vegetable stock in small portions and reduce while stirring, then add the stock again and reduce again while stirring. When about half the vegetable stock is used up, add the capers. When the rice is cooked and has absorbed all of the broth, stir in the almond butter and yeast flakes.
3. Finally, stir in the lemon zest, fennel green, and basil. Season with pepper, lemon juice, and, if desired, a pinch of salt to taste. Garnish with fennel greens.

Preparation time: 15 minutes

Cooking/Baking time: 15 minutes

Serving: 3

INGREDIENTS

- 6th Tomatoes)
- 1 can Kidney beans
- 2 Onion (noun)
- 1 tbsp Peanut butter, creamy
- 2 Tea spoons Sambal Oelek
- 1 teaspoon cumin
- 2 Garlic cloves)
- salt
- Rapeseed oil

PREPARATION

1. Steam the diced onions in oil until translucent. Roughly dice tomatoes and add. Cook for 5 to 10 minutes, or until the tomatoes are soft.

2. Add cumin, peanut butter (be sure to use the "creamy" version), sambal oelek, drained beans, finely sliced garlic and salt. Simmer for 3 minutes over low heat. Rice or couscous tastes good with it.

MONKEY-BURGER

Preparation time: 40 minutes

Cooking/Baking time: 10 minutes

Serving: 4

INGREDIENTS

- 250 g Smoked tofu
- 50 g peanuts
- 4th Burger bun
- 2 Banana (noun)
- 2 tbsp soy sauce
- peanut butter
- 2 tbsp Sesame paste
- 1 Onion (noun)
- 1 Garlic cloves)
- 50 g flour
- sugar
- salt and pepper
- 1 Beefsteak tomato
- ½ Cucumber
- n. B Iceberg lettuce

- 1 tbsp mustard

PREPARATION

1. Chop half a banana, the onion, the peanuts, and the garlic finely. Mix in a bowl with the flour, mustard, soy sauce and sesame paste. Crumble the smoked tofu into small pieces, season with salt and pepper. Knead everything well until you get a nice mass. Form 4 burger patties out of it and dust them with a little flour on both sides.
2. Heat the oil in a large pan and fry the patties on both sides until they are crispy. Be careful when turning, because they are not quite as stable, especially at the beginning.
3. At the same time, caramelize the sugar in a pan if you like. Meanwhile, cut the remaining bananas into thin slices and add to the saucepan once the sugar has caramelized. Turn off the stove and take out the bananas.
4. Roast burger buns (in the oven or on the toaster). Then spread peanut butter as you like. Stack the iceberg lettuce, sliced tomatoes and cucumber as desired, place the patty on top. If you want, add more peanut butter (mhhhh!) And, last but not least, the caramelized bananas. Put the lid on and serve.

SPINACH STRUDEL WITH SUN-DRIED TOMATOES AND WALNUTS

Preparation time: 30 minutes

Cooking/Baking time: 20 minutes

Serving: 2

INGREDIENTS

- 1 roll (s) Puff pastry, square
- 8th Tomato (s), dried in oil
- 1 handful Walnuts
- 2 Garlic cloves)
- Some olive oil
- 200 g Spinach leaves, fresh
- 1 Onion (noun)
- Some Vegetable stock to deglaze
- salt and pepper

PREPARATION

1. Put the tomatoes, walnuts, a clove of garlic and a good dash of olive oil in a blender and make a pesto. Season with salt and pepper.
2. Deglaze with a little vegetable stock after sautéing onion and garlic in a little olive oil in a pan until translucent. Then add the spinach and cook for a few minutes until it collapses. Season with salt and pepper.

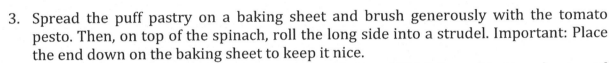

3. Spread the puff pastry on a baking sheet and brush generously with the tomato pesto. Then, on top of the spinach, roll the long side into a strudel. Important: Place the end down on the baking sheet to keep it nice.

4. Brush the puff pastry with a little water and bake at 200 ° C top / bottom heat until golden brown. This takes approximately 20 minutes. Of course, a garlic dip or a tomato sauce are optional; however, we also enjoyed it without them.

MY CREAMY, VEGAN PEANUT PAN WITH VEGETABLES AND SOY

Preparation time: 30 minutes

Cooking/Baking time: 20 minutes

Serving: 2

INGREDIENTS

- ¾ cup Soy granules
- n. B Vegetable stock, hot, to soak
- 1 m large Onion (s), diced
- 1 Garlic clove (s), crushed
- ½ m Size Carrot (s), diced
- ½ m Size Zucchini, diced
- 1 can Corn, (or 140 g vegetable corn)
- 100 ml Vegetable broth, strong
- 150 ml Soy milk (soy drink)
- 3 tbsp soy sauce
- 3 tbsp peanut butter
- 1 tbsp parsley
- Some Chili powder
- Some pepper
- Possibly. Curry powder

- Possibly. Paprika powder
- Some Vegetable oil, for frying
- Possibly. Flour, to thicken

PREPARATION

1. Put soy granules in a bowl. Bring the vegetable stock to the boil and pour over the granules. It should not lie "dry" and be able to swell well. Allow at least 5 minutes for it to swell. Then squeeze it out thoroughly and season with salt or broth as needed. It can taste nice and strong.
2. Heat the vegetable oil in the pan and add the granules. In my opinion, the best taste is achieved if you let the granules simmer properly until they are really nicely browned and crispy.
3. Then add the diced onions, carrots and the crushed clove of garlic and brown lightly. Finally, add the diced zucchini and corn.
4. Deglaze everything with a mixture of the soy milk, the strong vegetable stock and soy sauce. Add the peanut butter (I prefer it very creamy and add 4 large heaped tablespoons), as well as pepper and chili powder.
5. Cover the pan and leave it to cook until the zucchini is tender. If it's too thick, thin it out with soy milk or water. Finally, season with salt and pepper to taste.
6. The sauce should be creamy and flavorful, with a good amount of heat. If needed, season with broth, salt, chili powder, or pepper. Of course, you can thicken it with a little flour if you prefer. A sprig of fresh parsley rounds out the dish. I also have rice with it. If you like, you can also choose other side dishes.

SWEET PANCAKES VEGAN

Preparation time: 10 minutes

Cooking/Baking time: 15 minutes

Serving: 1

INGREDIENTS

- 1 cup Apple juice, clear or naturally cloudy *
- 2 Tea spoons baking powder
- 2 cup / n wheat flour
- 2 Tea spoons Syrup, brown, or sugar, or other sweetener
- 1 cup Soy milk (soy drink)
- 1 pinch (s) salt
- Vegetable fat, for frying

PREPARATION

1. Mix the baking powder with the flour. Use a whisk or blender to process all ingredients into a smooth dough.
2. Heat some fat in a pan and add enough dough with a ladle. Spread in the pan by swirling. On a medium setting, bake for 2 - 3 minutes on each side. Serve with powdered sugar, fruit, jam, nut-nougat cream or something similar.

Preparation time: 20 minutes

Cooking/Baking time: 35 minutes

Serving: 2

INGREDIENTS

- 2 Sweet potato
- 2 Beetroot
- 2 Parsley root
- 2 Parsnip (noun)
- 2 Carrot
- 6th Shallot (noun)
- 2 Garlic cloves)
- 3 branch / s   rosemary
- 3 branch / s   thyme
- salt and pepper
- 3 tbsp olive oil

FOR THE SET:

- some stems Parsley, smooth

PREPARATION

1. Preheat the oven to 200°F on both the top and bottom racks. Except for the garlic and shallots, wash and peel the vegetables before cutting them into bite-sized but not too small pieces. Peel the shallots rather than chopping them. Unpeeled garlic cloves are used.

2. Combine the vegetables, herbs, salt, pepper, and olive oil on a baking sheet. If possible, arrange the beets separately on the edge to avoid discoloring the other vegetables. Bake for 35 minutes on the middle rack of the oven. Turn the vegetables over and over so that they are evenly roasted. Serve sprinkled with the chopped parsley.

PUMPKIN AND SPINACH CURRY

Preparation time: 30 minutes

Cooking/Baking time: 15 minutes

Serving: 2

INGREDIENTS

- 1 smaller Butternut squash (se) (butternut)
- 400 g Spinach, fresh
- 1 Onion (noun)
- 1 Garlic cloves)
- 1 piece (s) Ginger, 1 cm or more, to taste
- 1 Chilli, fresh or flakes, amount according to heat and taste
- 2 Tea spoons Curry powder, amount according to heat and taste
- Some Cumin powder
- 2 tbsp Oil, neutral
- 200 ml Coconut milk
- 200 ml Vegetable broth
- salt and pepper
- some Lemon juice

PREPARATION

1. Remove the seeds from the pumpkin and dice the pulp. Wash the spinach and remove the thick stalks. Peel onion and garlic and chop finely. Peel and grate the ginger. Core and finely dice the chilli pepper.
2. Heat the oil, sauté the onion and garlic in it, add the curry, ginger, chilli and cumin and sweat, then add the pumpkin cubes. Deglaze with the vegetable stock and simmer for about ten minutes, until the pumpkin is almost done.
3. Fold in coconut milk and spinach and heat. The spinach should just collapse. Season with salt, pepper, and lemon juice, to taste.

FENNEL-CHICORY-RADICCHIO SALAD

Preparation time: 15 minutes
Cooking/Baking time: 0 minutes
Serving: 4

INGREDIENTS

- 1 bulb / n Fennel, with green
- 2 Chicory
- 1 Radicchio, small
- 3 tbsp Walnuts, roasted, roughly chopped
- 3 tbsp Pomegranate seeds
- For the dressing:
- 1 tbsp Grenadine
- 3 tbsp Vegetable broth, cooled
- salt and pepper
- 1 tbsp Oil, neutral

PREPARATION

1. Wash the fennel, cut in half and remove the stalk. Put the greens aside. Slice the fennel thinly or cut into strips. Wash the chicory stalk without cutting it into bite-sized pieces. Reduce the size of the radicchio leaves. Combine everything except the walnuts and pomegranate seeds in a mixing bowl.
2. To make the dressing, combine all of the ingredients except the oil in a mixing bowl. Finally whip in the oil vigorously, season the dressing to taste and fold into the salad. Before serving, pour the fennel greens (plucked into "flags") over the salad.

Preparation time: 20 minutes
Cooking/Baking time: 15 minutes
Serving: 2

INGREDIENTS

- 2 Garlic cloves)
- 1 small Onion (noun)
- 1 Chilli pepper (s), red
- 2 tbsp olive oil
- some thyme
- 1 tbsp oregano
- Some salt
- 1 tbsp Olives, black, black
- 1 tbsp Capers
- 1 can Tomatoes, chunky
- 200 g spaghetti

PREPARATION

1. Peel and finely chop the garlic and onion cloves. Wash the chilli pepper and cut into fine slices.
2. Heat the olive oil and lightly fry the processed ingredients. Season with thyme, oregano and salt. Add the olives, capers and the chopped tomatoes. Put the lid on the pan and let it simmer.
3. In the meantime, heat the salted water in a saucepan, add the olive oil and a little salt and cook the spaghetti in it.

EGGPLANT ROLLS VEGAN

Preparation time: 30 minutes

Cooking/Baking time: 15 minutes

Serving: 4

INGREDIENTS

- 1 large Eggplant (s) or 2 small ones
- 2 tbsp olive oil
- 3 large Onion (s) or 4 medium-sized ones
- 2 Garlic cloves)
- 12th Tomato (s), dried in oil
- 12th Olives
- 200 g Tomato paste
- n. B salt and pepper
- n. B Garlic pepper
- 1 branch / s   rosemary
- 4 branch / s   oregano
- 1 branch / s   thyme

PREPARATION

1. Cut the eggplant into thin slices. Fry on both sides with a little olive oil. While one side of the eggplants is frying, season the other side with salt, pepper, and garlic pepper. Now also add the fresh herbs. Now turn the aubergines and season on the other side.

2. Cut the onions into slices and the garlic. Add the onions to the pan. It is best to put it on the edge. When the eggplants are done roasted, place them on a plate. Now distribute the onions in the pan and add tomato paste. Let roast briefly. Then add fresh oregano to the pan and season with salt and pepper if necessary.

3. Then brush the aubergines with the onion mixture. Add the sun-dried tomatoes and roll up like a roulade. Finally, add a wooden skewer and an olive to finish. Garnish with a little chopped parsley or rocket.

4. As an alternative to the grill pan I used, the aubergines can also be prepared in the oven. Put some olive oil, garlic, rosemary and thyme on the baking sheet. Then place the aubergines on top and cook in the oven at 250 ° C. Again, it is best to turn the aubergines once and season with salt and pepper.

VEGAN SPINACH CASHEW LASAGNA

Preparation time: 30 minutes

Cooking/Baking time: 50 minutes

Serving: 4

INGREDIENTS

- 1 m large Onion (noun)
- 1 kg Spinach leaves, TK
- 150 ml water
- 70 g Cashews
- 1 toe / n garlic
- ½ tsp salt and pepper
- 0.33 tsp nutmeg
- 1 pinch Chili powder or cayenne pepper
- 1 pck Soy cream (soy cream cuisine)
- 150 g Cashew nuts or almonds
- 500 ml Water, hot
- 1 tbsp food starch
- ½ pck Lasagne plate (s)
- 4 large Tomatoes)
- 50 ml water

- Some oil

PREPARATION

1. Cut the onion into cubes, roughly chop 70 g cashew nuts and cut the tomatoes into slices. Preheat the oven to 180 ° C fan oven. Cook the onions in a little oil until softened, then add the spinach and 150 ml water and cook until the spinach is thawed.
2. In the meantime, roast the coarsely chopped cashew nuts in a pan without fat. In a blender, puree the garlic, salt, pepper, nutmeg, chilli, soy cream, 150 g cashew nuts or almonds and cornstarch with 500 ml hot water until you have a homogeneous mass without pieces.
3. Then the lasagna is layered: Put about 50 ml of water and a dash of oil on the bottom of the baking dish so that the pasta does not stick to the form. Then layer the lasagna sheets, spinach, a little sauce and roasted cashew nuts and again layer the lasagna sheets until the spinach is used up. Spread the tomatoes on the top layer of pasta and pour the rest of the sauce over it.
4. Place in the oven for approx. 40 - 45 minutes, until the noodles are soft and a light brown layer has formed.

Preparation time: 15 minutes
Cooking/Baking time: 30 minutes
Serving: 2

INGREDIENTS

- 500 g Potatoes)
- 500 g Beans, (bush), green
- 125 g Smoked tofu
- 400 ml Vegetable broth
- 1 large Onion (noun)
- 1 tbsp mustard
- 1 shot vinegar
- Some Oil, for frying
- salt
- Pepper, freshly ground
- n. B Savory

PREPARATION

1. Wash, peel and cut the potatoes into cubes as thick as a thumb. Wash the beans, cut off the ends and cut into bite-sized pieces. Cut the onion and smoked tofu into fine cubes.
2. Fry the onions and tofu in hot oil. Add the potatoes and beans and turn several times with the onions and tofu. Season well with salt and pepper and deglaze with vegetable stock. Add savory if you like. With the lid closed, simmer for 20 minutes, until the beans and potatoes are cooked through. Stir occasionally. Add the vinegar

about 15 minutes before the end of the cooking time. Season with mustard, salt, and pepper to taste, and serve.

VIETNAMESE SUMMER ROLLS

Preparation time: 30 minutes

Cooking/Baking time: 40 minutes

Serving: 4

INGREDIENTS

- 150 g Glass noodles
- 2 Shallot (noun)
- 2 toe / n garlic
- Oil, preferably peanut oil
- 2 Tea spoons Curry paste, as hot as possible
- 2 tbsp soy sauce
- 250 g Smoked tofu
- 100 g Carrot
- ½ Iceberg lettuce
- 1 Avocado (s)
- 1 bunch Coriander, fresh
- n. B Dough sheets, (rice sheets), large, from the Asian store
- peanut butter

PREPARATION

1. Pour boiling water over the glass noodles, let them steep and drain. Put them in a bowl and cut them a few times with scissors. They should be "handy".
2. Chop the shallots and garlic into small pieces. Heat with oil in a pan. Add the curry paste and sweat with it. Pour the soy sauce on, simmer gently, add to the glass noodles and mix. Season to taste, it should taste nice and spicy. Only then is it correct in the roles afterwards. Let cool down.
3. Crumble the smoked tofu in a bowl as best you can and fry it until crispy in a pan. Let cool down. Peel and roughly grate the carrots. Chop the lettuce into small pieces. Peel the avocado and cut into thin strips. Either or chop the coriander and mix it with the glass noodles.
4. For the rolls: Moisten a kitchen towel, wring it out and place on a large board. Put all the ingredients close at hand next to the board. Now moisten a rice sheet under the tap or in a bowl with water and then place it on the cloth. First place the coriander leaves in the middle so that they create a nice pattern.
5. Spread a strip of peanut butter next to it. Then put the grated carrots on top. A 3 cm edge at the bottom and a little more at the top is required. Add the salad just before the edge at the bottom to about the middle, followed by the glass noodle mixture. Finally, and this can also be distributed roughly, add the tofu. Fold down the bottom edge and the page on the right with care. Now roll up tightly but carefully.
6. Repeat this over and over and try different techniques until you have found the best one for you. A peanut dip, sweet and sour sauce or the typical summer roll sauce taste very delicious.

POTATO AND BRUSSELS SPROUTS GRATIN

Preparation time: 30 minutes

Cooking/Baking time: 45 minutes

Serving: 4

INGREDIENTS

- 1 ½ kg Potatoes)
- 1 kg Brussels sprouts
- 300 g Mushrooms, brown
- 250 g   Cheese, grated, vegan (pizza melt)
- 200 ml Soy cream (soy cream cuisine), for cooking
- 75 g Margarine, vegan
- 1 large Onion (noun)
- 1 teaspoon, heaped   Oregano, rubbed
- 1 teaspoon Cumin powder
- TL, st Nutmeg, freshly grated
- Rapeseed oil
- salt
- water

PREPARATION

1. The potatoes and Brussels sprouts should be peeled or cleaned and washed. Cut the Brussels sprouts in half, leaving the small florets intact and only cutting a small amount off the stem. Cut the potatoes into similar-sized pieces; otherwise, larger potato pieces will require more cooking time. Cook the potatoes and Brussels sprouts for about 15-20 minutes in salted water.

2. Clean the mushrooms and cut into cubes about 1 cm x 1 cm. Cut or chop the peeled onion into small cubes and sauté together with the mushrooms in rapeseed oil for about 10 minutes in a large pan.

3. Mix the pizza melt with the cooking cream and the spices, adding the amount of salt to taste. Rapeseed oil should be used to grease a casserole dish (s) that is large enough or divided into portions. Place the potatoes and Brussels sprouts evenly in the baking dish and pour over the steamed mushrooms and onions. Spread the vegetable margarine in flakes over the vegetables. Pour the cooking cream pizza melt evenly over the vegetables and grill everything at 200 ° C top / bottom heat or circulating air 180 ° C for 15 to 20 minutes.

CIG KÖFTE

Preparation time: 15 minutes

Cooking/Baking time: 40 minutes

Serving: 4

INGREDIENTS

- 2 cups Bulgur for "Cig Köfte", finely ground, approx. 300 g in total
- n. B water
- 2 Onion (noun)
- 2 toe / n garlic
- 2 tbsp Paprika pulp
- 2 tbsp Tomato paste
- 2 tbsp olive oil
- 4 tbsp Parsley, freshly chopped
- salt and pepper
- n. B Chili powder, spicy (at least 1 teaspoon)
- 1 tbsp Pomegranate syrup
- Some Lemon juice
- n. B Lettuce (e.g. iceberg lettuce)

PREPARATION

1. Pour hot water over the bulgur (cover just enough), close with a lid and allow to swell. In the meantime, grate the onions and chop the parsley.
2. Put all ingredients in a large bowl and knead everything well. Kneading is a very long story - it should take about 20 minutes. By kneading the bulgur becomes very fine and you can shape delicious meatballs.
3. Place the ingredients in the food processor and turn it on. Then, with your own hands, knead the rest of the fine work.
4. (Traditional) Serving Suggestion: Serve Cig Köfte with fresh, crunchy lettuce leaves so that you can wrap your meatball in this lettuce leaf. The sharpness of the Cig Köfte is slightly offset by the freshness of the lettuce leaf. A few drops of lemon juice or pomegranate syrup on top - delicious!

SWEET POTATO CURRY WITH CARAMELIZED PINEAPPLE

Preparation time: 25 minutes

Cooking/Baking time: 20 minutes

Serving: 4

INGREDIENTS

- 700 g Sweet potato
- 2 Carrot
- 2 zucchini
- ½ Pineapple, fresh
- 1 Onion (s), red
- 250 ml Coconut milk
- 1 stick / n Spring onions)
- 1 piece (s) Ginger, fresh, about the size of a walnut
- 1 pinch (s) Sugar, brown
- 1 small Chilli, red
- 50 g Flaked almonds
- 1 tbsp Curry powder
- n. B salt
- 1 tbsp peanut oil
- n. B Pepper from the grinder

PREPARATION

1. Peel and roughly dice half a pineapple. Fry until golden brown in a nonstick pan. Remove from the pan, season with milled black pepper, and set aside.
2. Peel the sweet potatoes and carrots and cut into approx. 1.5 cm thick cubes or slices. Finely dice the onion. Wash the zucchini well, cut into thick slices and then cut in half or quarter. Finely grate the ginger. Cut the chilli into fine rings.
3. Then heat the oil in a large saucepan and lightly roast sweet potatoes and carrots in it, roast zucchini and onions as well, so that a light roasted aroma is created. Then pour in coconut milk, stir in ginger and chilli and bring to the boil, then simmer on a lower flame and stir in the curry powder.
4. In the meantime, toast the flaked almonds in a pan without fat. Slowly, because when it burns, it tastes bitter. Cut the spring onion into fine rings and set both aside.
5. Season the curry with salt, fresh black pepper and a pinch of brown sugar. Arrange in deep plates or bowls. Drape the pineapple on the curry, sprinkle with the flaked almonds and the spring onion rings. Serve hot.

SWEET AND SOUR TOFU PAN WITH PINEAPPLE AND SPRING ONION

Preparation time: 15 minutes

Cooking/Baking time: 15 minutes

Serving: 4

INGREDIENTS

- 400 g tofu
- 4 tbsp Soy sauce, vegan
- 3 tbsp food starch
- Some Oil for frying
- 1 bunch Spring onions)
- 1 glass Pineapple in its own juice (350 g)
- 1 Garlic cloves)
- 1 tbsp Apple cider vinegar, vegan
- 1 piece (s) Ginger root, 2 cm
- 2 tbsp food starch
- 5 tbsp Water, cold
- 50 g Cashews

PREPARATION

1. Dice the tofu and pour the soy sauce over it. Let marinate for at least 30 minutes. Remove the tofu cubes from the soy sauce, drain thoroughly and dust with 3 tablespoons of cornstarch. Heat the frying oil in a large pan and fry the tofu cubes in it. Remove the tofu from the pan and keep it warm.
2. Drain the pineapple pieces and collect the juice. Cut the spring onions into fine rings and place in the hot pan with the pineapple pieces. Steam for a few minutes.
3. Meanwhile, finely chop the ginger and garlic and mix with the rest of the soy sauce, apple cider vinegar and about 4 tablespoons of pineapple juice. Deglaze the spring onions and the pineapple pieces with this sauce.
4. Mix 2 tablespoons of cornstarch with the cold water until lump-free and add to the pan. Heat everything, stirring constantly, until the sauce begins to boil and thickens.
5. Finally, sprinkle with cashews, season with soy sauce, pineapple juice, or vinegar to taste, and serve immediately. Basmati rice goes well with it.

Preparation time: 20 minutes

Cooking/Baking time: 1 hour 5 minutes

Serving: 4

INGREDIENTS

FOR THE PATTIES:

- 200 g Azuki beans, dried or 600 g canned, alternatively kidney beans
- 1 m large Onion (noun)
- n. B Rapeseed oil
- 2 tbsp mustard
- n. B salt and pepper
- n. B Spice (s) (oregano, paprika powder, chili powder, herbs of Provence)
- 1 Garlic cloves)
- 100 g breadcrumbs
- Oil for frying

ASIDE FROM THAT:

- 4th Burger buns (e.g. wholemeal buns for toasting)
- 4 sheets Leaf lettuce

- 4 slice / n Cucumber
- 4 slice / n Tomatoes)
- n. B cress
- ½ Bell pepper (noun)
- 8 tbsp Ketchup or BBQ sauce

PREPARATION

1. Soak the azuki beans in plenty of water overnight. Then cook for 50 minutes without salt. Meanwhile, chop an onion into small pieces and fry it. Season the beans, then top with the fried onions.
2. Now toast the buns. Now add the mustard, spices and garlic to the beans and knead vigorously. Add the breadcrumbs, the beans must break open. Shape the meatballs out of this and fry them in a little rapeseed oil. Finish the burger with lettuce, tomato, cucumber, paprika, cress and ketchup or BBQ sauce.

VEGAN SAUCE À LA CARBONARA

Preparation time: 5 minutes

Cooking/Baking time: 10 minutes

Serving: 2

INGREDIENTS

- 4 tbsp Yeast flakes
- 3 tsp flour
- 1 teaspoon salt
- 1 pinch (s) Paprika powder
- 1 pinch (s) pepper
- 1 teaspoon mustard
- 150 ml Soy drink
- 3 toe / n garlic
- ½ Onion (noun)
- 75 g Smoked tofu
- n. B Soy cream (soy cream cuisine)
- 4 tbsp oil

PREPARATION

1. Heat the oil in the saucepan, dice the onions and garlic and fry in the fat until translucent. Cut the smoked tofu into cubes, add and fry on medium heat until crispy. Mix the first 5 ingredients together and mix with the ingredients in the pot with a whisk.
2. Now add the mustard and sweat everything briefly, stirring constantly. Add the soy drink and bring to the boil. A viscous mass is created. Finally, the desired consistency / creaminess can be achieved with the soy cream (I take about 1/3 or 1/4 from a 250ml package).

SPAGHETTI WITH VEGAN SPINACH SOUR CREAM

Preparation time: 30 minutes

Cooking/Baking time: 10 minutes

Serving: 3

INGREDIENTS

- 500 g spaghetti
- 450 g Spinach leaves, TK
- 1 m large Onion (noun)
- 3 toe / n garlic
- 4 tbsp olive oil
- 100 ml water
- nutmeg
- salt and pepper
- Paprika powder
- Chili powder
- 1 teaspoon Pine nuts

FOR THE CREAM:

- 100 ml Soy milk (soy drink), 3% protein content min.
- 50 ml Vegetable oil

- 1 tbsp Lemon juice
- 2 pinches Guar gum
- salt and pepper

PREPARATION

1. Vegan Sour Cream: Put the soy drink with the oil, lemon juice, 2 teaspoon tips of guar gum and salt and pepper in a tall container and beat with the hand blender for 2 minutes until it thickens and then refrigerate for at least 1 hour.
2. In a hot pan, toast the pine nuts without using any oil. Cook the spaghetti according to the package directions.
3. Cook the onion in hot olive oil with the garlic until it is translucent. Cook for 5 minutes on medium heat with the thawed spinach and 100 ml water. Season with nutmeg, pepper, salt, paprika, and a pinch of cayenne pepper.
4. Fold in the sour cream, let it steep for another 5 minutes on a low level and add seasoning if necessary. Sprinkle the sauce with the roasted seeds and serve with the spaghetti.

KETOGENIC DIET

The ketogenic diet is a high-fat diet that has gained popularity in recent years. However, it has been used to treat certain pathologies, including epilepsy, for nearly a century. The goal of this diet is to drastically reduce carbohydrate intake in favor of fat in order to induce ketosis. Aside from the significant weight loss, there would be numerous health benefits.

FEATURES OF THE KETOGENIC DIET:

- ❖ Lipid consumption is extremely high (75 percent of intakes)
- ❖ Unchanged protein intake
- ❖ Considerable reduction in carbohydrate intake
- ❖ Rapid weight loss
- ❖ The ketosis state would have numerous health benefits (energy boost, protection against certain pathologies, etc.)

HOW DOES THE KETOGENIC DIET AID IN WEIGHT LOSS?

Typically, the body obtains its energy from the carbohydrates consumed during the day, which are required for the body's proper functioning. Because carbohydrates are extremely limited on the ketogenic diet, the body begins to draw on its stores of carbohydrates stored in the muscles and liver known as "glycogen stores." Because each gram of glycogen in the body is bound to 3-4g of water, the significant weight loss at the start of the ketogenic diet is largely due to water loss. When glycogen stores are depleted, the body switches to using lipids or fat for energy. When the body uses fat in the absence of carbohydrates, however, it produces waste products known as ketones. Following that, ketones begin to accumulate in the blood, and their odor, which resembles nail polish, becomes noticeable on the breath. It is the primary indicator that the body is in "ketosis". It typically takes 2 to 4 weeks to reach this point. You can test for "ketosis" by purchasing urine test strips from a pharmacy.

This "ketosis" state causes a significant decrease in appetite, which aids in reducing the amount of food consumed. This condition can also cause nausea and exhaustion. Although this diet does not emphasize calorie counting, those who adhere to it consume fewer calories because they are not hungry, resulting in weight loss. There is no time limit on the ketogenic weight loss diet. When used in the therapeutic field, the ketogenic diet can last anywhere from a few weeks to several years, depending on the desired outcome.

KETOGENIC DIET APPROVED FOODS

Significant amounts of the following foods are permitted on the ketogenic diet:

- ❖ Pisces

- ❖ Sea food
- ❖ Meat
- ❖ Poultry
- ❖ Eggs
- ❖ Butter
- ❖ Vegetal oils
- ❖ Vinegar
- ❖ Lemon juice
- ❖ Olives
- ❖ Lawyer
- ❖ Low-carb vegetables (spinach, lettuce, kale, etc.)
- ❖ Hard cheese (100 g per day)

Foods that are permitted but should be consumed in moderation include:

- ❖ Whole milk
- ❖ Whole milk yogurts
- ❖ Vegetables with a higher carbohydrate content (except carrots, beets, sweet potatoes, peas and corn)
- ❖ Wine
- ❖ Strong alcohol
- ❖ Coffee without sugar

Because a significant amount of fat is consumed each day, it is critical to be mindful of the type of fat consumed. It is best to limit your intake of omega-6 fatty acids, which have a pro-inflammatory effect when consumed in excess. Soybean, corn, safflower, grape seed, sunflower, and wheat germ oils are the most abundant sources of omega-6. As a result, salad dressings, dressings, and mayonnaise made with these oils should be consumed in moderation. It is preferable to consume monounsaturated fats (olive oil, avocado, nuts) rather than saturated fats (fatty cuts of meat, high-fat dairy products). Coconut oil is advised to be used because it contains fats that are easily converted into ketones. Finally, Omega-3 fatty fish, rapeseed and flaxseed oil, walnuts, or even chia, flax, or hemp seeds must be consumed in sufficient quantities.

PROHIBITED FOODS

The ketogenic diet is relatively restrictive; many foods are forbidden because they prevent the body from staying in ketosis:

- ❖ Sugar
- ❖ Sweet products
- ❖ Cereals
- ❖ Starchy
- ❖ Bread
- ❖ Pastries
- ❖ Pastries

- ❖ Biscuits
- ❖ Legumes
- ❖ Fruits (except berries)
- ❖ Potato
- ❖ Sweet vegetables (beets, corn, carrots, etc.)
- ❖ Soft-paste cheese
- ❖ cream cheese
- ❖ Soft drinks
- ❖ Chocolate
- ❖ Honey, jams, syrup
- ❖ Fruit and vegetable juices
- ❖ Sweet sauces
- ❖ Vegetable milk-based milk or yogurt (soya, almonds, etc.)
- ❖ Flavored yogurts
- ❖ Sweet fruit compotes

ADVANTAGES AND DISADVANTAGES

- ❖ Feeling full
- ❖ No calorie restriction
- ❖ Good supply of quality lipids and proteins
- ❖ Rapid weight loss
- ❖ Potentially positive effect on blood lipid levels

THE NEGATIVES OF THE KETO DIET

- ❖ In the first few weeks, there may be some unpleasant side effects (ketogenic flu)
- ❖ Little dietary diversity
- ❖ No deviation allowed
- ❖ Difficult to follow
- ❖ Monotone
- ❖ Not very conducive to a fulfilling social life

RECOMMENDATIONS AND PRECAUTIONS TO BE TAKEN

WHAT ARE THE DANGERS OF THE KETOGENIC DIET?

Very unpleasant side effects can occur in the first few weeks. The ketogenic flu is what we're talking about. It is a transitional period that almost always coincides with the passage of the organism through ketosis. Be cautious; some side effects, such as hypoglycemia (low blood sugar level), dehydration, an increased risk of urolithiasis or kidney stones, and constipation, appear to persist even after the transition period.

IS IT A DIET THAT IS SUITABLE FOR BODYBUILDING AND SPORTS?

Yes, exactly. Some studies even show that the ketogenic diet has benefits such as improved performance, reduced recovery time, and ease of exertion. This diet has become very popular in the sports world in recent years.

HOW CAN I AVOID GAINING WEIGHT?

The ketogenic diet is more of a way of life than a diet. As a result, it should not be abandoned after a few months. However, given the severe restrictions it imposes, it appears that gaining weight is unavoidable if it is discontinued. To avoid a yo-yo effect, it would appear beneficial to be accompanied by a nutrition professional who could help gradually reintroduce carbohydrates into the diet without too severe consequences.

KETO RECIPES

LOW CARB KETO TARTE FLAMBÉE

Preparation time: 20 minutes

Cooking/Baking time: 30 minutes

Serving: 1

INGREDIENTS

- 120 g Quark
- 2 Egg (s)
- 160 g Cheese, grated
- 100 g Creme fraiche Cheese
- 2 Spring onion (s), cut into rolls
- 50 g Bacon cubes

PREPARATION

1. Preheat the oven to 170 ° C top / bottom. In a mixing bowl, combine the quark, eggs, and 80 g cheese for the base. Smooth the mixture out onto a baking sheet lined with parchment paper. Bake for 15 minutes at 350°F.

2.

3. Remove the baking sheet, coat the cake base with crème fraîche, and top with the bacon, spring onions, and remaining cheese. Bake for another 15-20 minutes, or until the cheese is nicely browned. Can be eaten as a tarte flambée or as a roll.

Preparation time: 2 minutes

Cooking/Baking time: 3 minutes

Serving: 1

INGREDIENTS

- 10 g butter
- 1 Egg (s)
- ½ tsp baking powder
- 30 g Almond flour

PREPARATION

1. Briefly liquefy the butter in the microwave. Stir together all of the ingredients in a standard coffee mug. Make sure that the dough is smooth and that there are really no lumps left (this leads to the formation of bubbles in the bread and ends with holes).
2. Now put the mug in the microwave for 90 seconds at full power. If the dough is still slightly moist (possibly possible with 600 watts), simply continue cooking in 10 second steps until it is firm. Tilt out of the cup immediately after cooking.

KETO SCRAMBLED EGGS

Preparation time: 10 minutes

Cooking/Baking time: 5 minutes

Serving: 1

INGREDIENTS

- 3 Egg (s)
- ¼ tsp salt
- ¼ tsp pepper
- ½ tsp Paprika powder, hot pink
- 1 teaspoon Chives, dried or freshly chopped
- 1 Tomatoes)
- 100 g   Bacon, diced into small pieces
- 1 handful Pizza cheese
- 1 tbsp Cream cheese (brunch paprika & pepperoni), optional

PREPARATION

1. Mix the eggs with the spices and chives. Cut the tomato into small cubes and add to the eggs along with the bacon, cheese and brunch and stir well again.
2. Fry in a pan as you like, some prefer scrambled eggs golden-brown, others rather loose and flaky, so proceed as you like. Protein bread with salami tastes good with it.

LOW CARB KETO CHOCOLATE PUDDING

Preparation time: 1 minute

Cooking/Baking time: 0 minutes

Serving: 1

INGREDIENTS

- 250 ml Whipped cream
- 200 g Mascarpone
- 1 tbsp, heaped Baked cocoa, 30 g
- 10 ml Liquid sweetener

PREPARATION

1. Put everything in a blender and let it run for 30 seconds until the cream is stiff. That's it. You can add a few nuts if you like.

Preparation time: 15 minutes

Cooking/Baking time: 20 minutes

Serving: 4

INGREDIENTS

- 600 g chicken breast
- 4th zucchini
- 1 Onion (noun)
- Coconut oil
- 1 can Coconut milk
- salt
- Cayenne pepper
- curry
- turmeric

PREPARATION

1. Finely chop the onions and cut the chicken breast into small cubes. Bring the zucchini into "pasta form". It works best with a spiral cutter.
2. Fry the chicken breast in coconut oil for a few minutes before adding the onions and cooking until they are translucent. Then pour coconut milk on top and season well with curry, turmeric, cayenne pepper and salt. The sauce should be nice and yellow and taste strong.

3. Let the sauce reduce a little and then add the zucchini and let it get hot. Arrange on plates and serve immediately.

LOW CARB KETO TARTE FLAMBÉE ROLLS

Preparation time: 15 minutes

Cooking/Baking time: 30 minutes

Serving: 1

INGREDIENTS

- 2 Egg (s)
- 120 g lowfat quark
- 130 g Cheese, grated, light
- 100 g Crème fraîche, alternatively crème lègére
- 1 bunch Spring onion (noun)
- 50 g Ham cubes
- n. B salt and pepper
- 1 tbsp Herbs or crème fraîche with herbs

PREPARATION

1. For the base, mix the low-fat quark with the eggs and 80 g cheese and stir until smooth. Season with salt and pepper to taste.
2. Put the liquid mixture on a baking sheet lined with baking paper and distribute it evenly. One portion is roughly enough for a tray, but it can vary slightly depending on the size of the oven. However, as is usual with a tarte flambée, the mixture can be spread very thinly.

3. Bake in the preheated oven at 175 ° C top / bottom heat or 160 ° C convection for about 15 minutes on the middle shelf until it turns a light golden brown color. Do not bake for too long, because the dough will come back into the oven after topping. If small bubbles form, just prick them with a fork so that the bottom stays nice and smooth. Once the desired brown color has been achieved, take the dough out of the oven and let it cool down for about 5 minutes.

4. Spread crème fraîche on the dough. If you like, you can season a little with salt and pepper. Sprinkle with the sliced spring onions, diced ham, and the remaining 50 g cheese. Put back in the oven on the middle rack for about 15 minutes until the cheese has melted and is slightly brown.

5. If you want, you can eat it as a low-carb tarte flambée or let the cake cool down briefly and carefully roll it up using the baking paper and cut it into bite-sized pieces.

LOW CARB CURD BREAD

Preparation time: 10 minutes

Cooking/Baking time: 60 minutes

Serving: 1

INGREDIENTS

- 2 large Egg (s)
- 500 g lowfat quark
- 300 g Almond (s), ground
- 50 g Chia seeds
- 5 g baking powder
- 1 teaspoon Flea seeds
- 1 teaspoon salt

PREPARATION

1. Mix all ingredients and bake at 180 degrees for about an hour.

Preparation time: 2 minutes

Cooking/Baking time: 5 minutes

Serving: 1

INGREDIENTS

- 180 g Ground beef
- 1 Tomatoes)
- 1 Avocado (s)
- 1 teaspoon, heaped   butter
- salt and pepper
- Paprika powder, noble sweet, smoked

PREPARATION

1. Fry the minced meat in a pan until crumbly. In the meantime, dice the tomato. Halve the avocado and remove the stone.
2. Add the butter to the minced meat and season to taste. With a coffee spoon, remove small pieces from the avocado halves and add to the minced meat in the pan. Season again to taste and add the diced tomato. Stir and serve immediately.

KETO OR LOW CARB ZUCCHINI PANCAKES WITH SMOKED SALMON AND GARLIC CRÈME FRAÎCHE

Preparation time: 15 minutes

Cooking/Baking time: 15 minutes

Serving: 3

INGREDIENTS

FOR THE BUFFERS:

- 3 zucchini
- 3 Egg (s)
- 1 tbsp Psyllium husks
- 3 tbsp Parmesan, grated
- 1 teaspoon salt and pepper
- Possibly. Spice (s) of your choice, optional

FOR THE DIP:

- 1 cup   Creme fraiche Cheese
- 2 toe / n garlic
- salt and pepper
- Aside from that:
- 200 g   smoked salmon

PREPARATION

1. Wash the zucchini, grate it finely and wring it out well in a kitchen towel so that as little liquid as possible remains. Then mix eggs, psyllium husks, parmesan, salt, pepper and, if necessary, spices to a homogeneous mass.
2. Let the oil or fat get hot in a pan and add small blobs of the mixture to the pan, depending on the size you want. Turning is the most difficult part as the buffers are very soft. Fry the first side a little longer so that it lasts better. The smaller the buffers, the easier it is.
3. For the dip, peel off 2 cloves of garlic, chop very finely and mix with the crème fraîche. Add salt and pepper to taste.
4. Arrange the finished pancakes on plates, cover with smoked salmon and top with a little crème fraîche.

Preparation time: 5 minutes

Cooking/Baking time: 50 minutes

Serving: 1

INGREDIENTS

- 200 g Ground almonds
- 1 tsp, leveled salt
- 3 Egg (s)
- 2 tbsp, heaped Psyllium husks
- 1 pck baking powder
- 200 ml Water, hot
- 2 tbsp, heaped Chia seeds

PREPARATION

1. Mix together the almond flour, salt, baking powder, chia seeds and psyllium husks. Add the eggs.
2. Mix well and then add hot but not boiling water and mix with the mixer. The mass is sticky at first, but then becomes easily malleable. Shape a small bread or roll with wet hands. Bake at 170 degrees Celsius for 40 to 50 minutes, depending on the size of the pan. As a variation, herbs, fried onions, caraway or cardamom can be added.

Preparation time: 15 minutes

Cooking/Baking time: 55 minutes

Serving: 1

INGREDIENTS

- 400 g Ground beef
- 300 g Carrot
- 100 g Tomato paste
- 600 ml Vegetable broth
- 2 m large Bell pepper (noun)
- 1 m large Onion (noun)
- 2 toe / n garlic
- 3 tbsp Crème fraîche or sour cream
- salt and pepper

PREPARATION

1. Fry the minced meat in a large saucepan. Chop the onion and garlic and add. Peel the carrots, cut into small slices and add to the minced meat. Fry everything for 5 minutes, stirring occasionally. Add tomato paste and mix well. Then deglaze with the broth, bring to the boil and simmer covered for 40 minutes over a low heat.

2. Cut the peppers into small sticks and add about 10 minutes before the end of the cooking time. Finally, season with salt and pepper. Place a dollop of crème fraîche on each plate.

LOW-CARB SALMON WITH ROASTED VEGETABLES

Preparation time: 15 minutes

Cooking/Baking time: 30 minutes

Serving: 2

INGREDIENTS

- 250 g   Salmon fillet (s), also frozen
- 100 g   Sheep cheese
- 1 m large zucchini
- 150 g   Mushrooms
- 1 m large Bell pepper (s), red or yellow
- 300 g   Cherry tomato (s) or tomato tomatoes
- 2 toe / n garlic
- some   salt and pepper
- some   Chili oil

PREPARATION

1. If frozen, let the salmon fillet thaw a little. Wash and pat dry. Season with salt and pepper to taste, as well as herbs if desired.

2. Cut the sheep's cheese into cubes. Thinly slice the zucchini and mushrooms, cut the peppers into strips. Halve or quarter the tomatoes. Finely chop the garlic. Mix the vegetables with the garlic, salt and pepper and a few dashes of chili oil in a bowl.

3. Form a "bowl" on a baking sheet made of aluminum foil *, ie fold up the edges on 4 sides. I recommend using 2 layers of aluminum foil, then nothing can leak. Then distribute the vegetables on top. Then place the salmon on top, drizzle with a little chilli oil and generously crumble the sheep's cheese over it. Cook in a hot oven at 180 ° C top / bottom heat for approx. 30 - 35 minutes.

ZUCCHINI LASAGNA

Preparation time: 40 minutes

Cooking/Baking time: 40 minutes

Serving: 4

INGREDIENTS

- 1 kg Zucchini, big, thick
- 1 large Onion (noun)
- 1Garlic cloves)
- 500 g Ground beef
- 1 tbsp Tomato paste
- 1 can Tomatoes, chunky
- 1 pck Cream cheese (200 g)
- 100 ml milk
- Possibly. Sour cream, optionally sour cream
- 150 g Cheese, grated
- olive oil
- salt and pepper
- Paprika powder, noble sweet
- oregano
- thyme

- Parsley, chopped

PREPARATION

1. Wash the zucchini and cut lengthways into finger-thick slices. Fry both sides in a pan in olive oil, then drain on kitchen paper. Or alternatively brush the slices with olive oil, add a little salt and brown on the top shelf using the grill function in the oven. However, it takes longer.

2. Cut the onion into cubes and sauté in a pan in a little olive oil until translucent. Squeeze the garlic clove and sauté a little. Fry the minced meat until it is crumbly. Season with salt, pepper, and paprika powder once the meat has turned color, then add 1 tablespoon tomato paste, stir, and sweat for a minute. Season the tomatoes with oregano, thyme, salt, pepper, and paprika. Simmer for 10 minutes on low heat before adding the chopped parsley.

3. Combine the cream cheese and milk in a mixing bowl; stir in the sour cream if desired. Season with salt, pepper and a little nutmeg, stir in approx. 50 g cheese.

4. Line a lasagne dish or other baking dish with zucchini slices. Spread a couple of spoons of tomato mince sauce on top, a layer of cream cheese sauce on top, and zucchini slices again. Keep layering until all of the ingredients have been used. The top layer should be tomato mince sauce. Sprinkle these with the rest of the cheese.

5. Bake the zucchini lasagne in a preheated oven at 200 ° C top / bottom heat for about 30 minutes until golden brown. It goes well with a small fresh salad.

Preparation time: 15 minutes

Cooking/Baking time: 15 minutes

Serving: 2

INGREDIENTS

- 500 g cauliflower
- 4 tbsp Double cream cheese
- 1 tbsp Butter or cream
- salt and pepper
- n. B nutmeg

PREPARATION

1. Divide the cauliflower into florets and place in well-salted water for 1/2 hour, any small animals that may be present will come out.
2. Then cook in a little fresh salted water for about 15 minutes until soft. Drain very well and puree with a hand blender while still hot or press through the potato press. Season with salt, pepper, and possibly nutmeg and combine with butter and cream cheese. Serve hot. It's especially good with a steak and fresh, crispy lettuce.

WRAPPED SALMON WITH BACON, SPICY STIR-FRIED VEGETABLES, AND FETA CHEESE

Preparation time: 15 minutes

Cooking/Baking time: 12 minutes

Serving: 1

INGREDIENTS

- 125 g Salmon fillet (s)
- 50 g Bacon
- 100 g broccoli
- 100 g Mushrooms
- 1 Onion (noun)
- 70 g zucchini
- 5 ml Peanut oil or olive oil
- 1 pinch (s) salt
- 1 pinch (s) pepper
- 1 pinch (s) Chilli flakes
- 1 pinch (s) Paprika powder
- 70 g Feta cheese or goat cheese or your choice
- 10 g Parmesan, grated

PREPARATION

1. Wash the salmon, pat dry and wrap completely in bacon. Clean / wash and cut broccoli, mushrooms, onions and zucchini.
2. Put a non-stick pan on medium heat and add the oil. Add the salmon with bacon and the prepared vegetables to the pan. Season the vegetables with salt, pepper, chilli flakes and paprika powder. Put the lid on. Shortly before the end of the roasting time (approx. 10 minutes) add the feta cheese to the vegetables. Then garnish and sprinkle the parmesan on the vegetables.

LOW-CARB CHICKEN BREAST IN A CREAMY CREAM CHEESE SAUCE WITH ZUCCHINI AND TOMATOES

Preparation time: 20 minutes

Cooking/Baking time: 30 minutes

Serving: 2

INGREDIENTS

- 250 g chicken breast
- 1 large zucchini
- ½ Cucumber
- 3 m large Vine tomato
- 2 small ones   Shallot (noun)
- 2 toe / n garlic
- 100 g   Cream cheese, low in fat, creamy finer
- 1 shot Milk, 1.5%
- salt and pepper
- Curry powder
- Paprika powder

PREPARATION

1. Clean and cut the chicken breast into bite-sized pieces. Fry the meat in a pan with a little vegetable fat until it's nice and crispy. Season with salt, pepper, and curry powder to taste.
2. Meanwhile, slice the zucchini, cucumber, and tomatoes into small pieces. Set aside the chicken and keep it warm.
3. Fry the onions and garlic in the same pan. Add zucchini and steam until they are soft but still firm to the bite. Add the cucumber and tomatoes and cook for about 4 minutes. Possibly add a dash of water.
4. Stir in the cream cheese and milk. Put the chicken in the pan and let the lid simmer over low heat for about 5 - 10 minutes until the sauce becomes creamy. Season to taste with paprika.

LOW CARB PIZZA

Preparation time: 15 minutes

Cooking/Baking time: 30 minutes

Serving: 2

INGREDIENTS

- 1 ½ can / n Tuna in its own juice
- 3 Egg (s)
- 2 slice / n cooked ham
- 80 g Cheese, grated, of your choice
- salt and pepper
- oregano
- Tomato sauce

PREPARATION

1. Mix two eggs well in a bowl. Drain the tuna, add to the eggs and mix everything well. Put the mixture on a baking sheet with parchment paper and shape it into a round shape. The bottom should be about 0.4-0.6 cm thick. Bake the tuna bottom in a preheated oven for 10-15 minutes at 180 ° C top / bottom heat.
2. Then take it out of the oven, brush with tomato sauce and season with salt, pepper and oregano. Tear the ham slices and cover the pizza with them. Sprinkle with cheese, crack open the third egg and place on the pizza.

3. Then put the pizza back in the oven and bake for about 20 minutes, until the egg is cooked and the cheese has a nice golden color. The pizza can of course also be topped differently according to taste.

THE BEST AND SIMPLEST LOW-CARB PIZZA, WITH A CREAM CHEESE, CHEESE, AND EGG BASE

Preparation time: 10 minutes

Cooking/Baking time: 40 minutes

Serving: 2

INGREDIENTS

FOR THE GROUND:

- 4th Egg (s)
- 200 g Cheese, grated
- 150 g cream cheese
- For covering:
- 100 g Tomato sauce, seasoned
- 100 g Mozzarella, grated
- n. B Vegetables and / or mushrooms
- n. B Salami or ham or other toppings

PREPARATION

1. Preheat the oven to 180°C top/bottom heat. Whisk together the cream cheese and eggs in a mixing bowl. Then stir in the grated cheese until well combined. Distribute the mixture evenly on the baking sheet - baking paper is advisable. Be careful, the dough is still relatively runny, but will firm up after baking.

2. Bake in the oven for about 30 minutes until golden brown. Then cover the base with tomato sauce, the desired toppings and mozzarella. Put in the oven for another 10 minutes.

Preparation time: 20 minutes

Cooking/Baking time: 20 minutes

Serving: 1

INGREDIENTS

- 55 g butter
- 30 g Dark chocolate or dark chocolate
- 40 g Cocoa powder
- 2 Egg (s), separated
- 150 g Sweetener (erythritol or xylitol)
- 70 g Almond flour, de-oiled
- ½ tsp baking powder
- 1 tsp, leveled Stevia powder, optional
- 1 vial Vanilla flavor

PREPARATION

1. Preheat the oven to 170 ° C top / bottom. Separate the eggs and fold in the egg whites. Melt the chocolate with the butter after breaking it up into smaller pieces (e.g. in the microwave or in a double boiler).
2. With the mixer, combine the cocoa powder and the remaining ingredients. Don't be surprised; the mass has solidified! Carefully fold in the egg whites. Pour the dough

into a 20 x 20 cm brownie pan (or a similar sized baking dish) and smooth it out. Bake in the hot oven for approx. 20 minutes.

BASIC RECIPE FOR LOW-CARB WRAP

Preparation time: 10 minutes

Cooking/Baking time: 20 minutes

Serving: 2

INGREDIENTS

- 100 g Quark
- 1 Egg (s)
- 100 g Cheese, grated
- 1 tbsp linseed

PREPARATION

1. Whisk the ingredients for the dough together and spread them on a baking sheet. Bake for 15 - 20 minutes, or until golden brown, at 180 ° C.
2. The filling can be designed as you like. I had the following in it: sliced gyros, mixed salad and tzatziki.

CHAFFLES

Preparation time: 2 minutes

Cooking/Baking time: 4 minutes

Serving: 2

INGREDIENTS

- 100 g Cheese, grated, e.g. B. mozzarella, cheddar or other cheeses
- 2 m large Egg (s)
- Some Oil for the waffle iron
- n. B salt and pepper

PREPARATION

1. Chaffles is derived from the English words Cheese (cheese) and Waffles (waffles) and that is exactly what they are: Cheese waffles. The variant with mozzarella is the basic recipe and, in my opinion, tastes the least cheesy.
2. Put the cheese in a bowl with the eggs and stir well until everything is smooth. If you like, you can now season with salt and pepper or add other ingredients to the chaffles.
3. Ham cubes are super delicious. Now fill the waffle iron (or a silicone waffle mold) with the mixture and bake. In the oven it takes about 15 minutes at 175 ° C.
4. The waffle iron is of course much faster, but requires the addition of oil. The cheese waffles are very suitable as a substitute for burger buns or can be topped up as sandwiches, but they also simply taste great.

KETO HAZELNUT COOKIES

Preparation time: 10 minutes

Cooking/Baking time: 12 minutes

Serving: 1

INGREDIENTS

- 75 g Ground hazelnuts
- ½ tsp baking powder
- 1 teaspoon, heaped   Protein powder
- 30 g Butter, melted
- 1 Egg (s)
- 30 g Erythritol (sugar substitute)

PREPARATION

1. Preheat the oven to 160 degrees Celsius (fan oven).
2. Make a dough out of all of the ingredients and place six small blobs on a baking sheet. Bake for 10 to 12 minutes, then remove from the oven and set aside to cool.

JUICY STRAWBERRY CAKE WITHOUT FLOUR AND SUGAR

Preparation time: 30 minutes

Cooking/Baking time: 30 minutes

Serving: 1

INGREDIENTS

- 80 g Butter (pasture butter) or ghee
- 4 large Egg (s) (organic)
- 1 pinch (s) sea-salt
- 15 g Xylitol (sugar substitute) for the soil
- 150 g Almond (s), ground
- 1 teaspoon, heaped   Vanilla powder (bourbon)
- 7 g Tartar baking powder
- 80 g cream
- 500 g Strawberries, ripe
- 1 pck Gelatin, red or icing
- 2 g Xylitol (sugar substitute) for the icing

PREPARATION

1. Preheat the oven to 180 degrees Celsius (top / bottom heat). Melt the butter or ghee gently.

2. Separate the eggs and beat the egg whites with a pinch of salt until stiff (overhead test). Beat the egg yolks with 15 g xylitol until frothy. Add the cream and butter while stirring. Mix the almonds with the vanilla and tartar and also add. Then carefully fold the egg white under the dough so that it stays fluffy.

3. Line the springform pan with baking paper and grease the edge well. Carefully pour in the dough, distribute it evenly and bake for about 30 minutes. Let the cake base cool down. You can bake the base the day before and store it in cling film in the refrigerator for further processing the next day.

4. Cut the cake base into 8 pieces. Wrap the edge of the springform pan with cling film and place it around the base as a "cake ring". Clean the strawberries, remove the greens and cut the fruit in half if necessary. Cover the cake base with it without covering the cut edges, so it can be easily cut again later.

5. Prepare gelatine or cake glaze with 2 g xylitol according to the package instructions. Distribute the mixture evenly over the strawberries. After the mixture has hardened, carefully remove the edge of the springform pan.

6. Chill the cake until ready to eat. Take out of the refrigerator 15 minutes beforehand to allow the aroma to develop. It goes well with whipped cream with fresh bourbon vanilla.

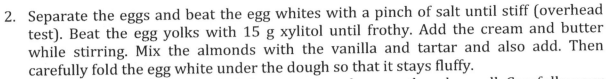

BAKED SALMON FILLET ON MUSHROOMS WITH A CRISPY SKIN

Preparation time: 5 minutes

Cooking/Baking time: 20 minutes

Serving: 2

INGREDIENTS

- 300 g   Salmon fillet (s) with skin
- 5 Mushrooms
- salt and pepper
- n. B Chili powder

PREPARATION

1. Wash the salmon fillet and pat dry with a kitchen roll. Place the fillet on the skin side and season the other side with ground salt, chilli or pepper.
2. Cut the mushrooms into slices and place in a baking dish. Place the salmon fillet on the mushrooms, skin side up. Sprinkle the skin with plenty of ground salt. Place the casserole dish in the oven and bake at 200 ° C for approx. 20-25 minutes until the skin is crispy and the salmon fillet is cooked through. A leaf spinach casserole or a green salad goes well with it.

Preparation time: 15 minutes

Cooking/Baking time: 35 minutes

Serving: 2

INGREDIENTS

- 300 g Kohlrabi, peeled and weighed
- 250 g Cauliflower, green or white
- 150 ml Almond milk (almond drink), unsweetened
- 50 g Camembert (s) (goat camembert) or other soft cheese, weighed without rind
- 25 g Ghee
- 50 g Parmesan
- n. B Pepper (Parisian pepper)
- n. B sea-salt

PREPARATION

1. Preheat the oven to 180° C top/bottom heat. Finely dice the peeled kohlrabi, use the fine florets of the cleaned cauliflower. Pre-cook them together for approx. 15 minutes so that the vegetables are still firm to the bite.
2. Meanwhile, gently heat the almond drink with ghee and the soft cheese without rind in a small saucepan until the cheese has melted. Then season the sauce to taste.
3. Spread the firm vegetables in a small baking dish. Spread the sauce evenly over the top. Cover evenly with the grated parmesan. Bake in the oven for about 20 minutes until the Parmesan cheese has turned lightly brown.

4. A light summer salad goes well with it, for example with dandelions, tomatoes and wild garlic feta.

SPINACH AND MINCED MEAT PIZZA OR CASSEROLE WITH GOAT CHEESE

Preparation time: 20 minutes

Cooking/Baking time: 45 minutes

Serving: 4

INGREDIENTS

FOR THE GROUND:

- 400 g   Ground beef, lean
- 1 tbsp Mustard, without sugar
- 2 Egg (s)
- 4 tsp Flour (macadamia nut flour), de-oiled
- 2 tbsp Parmesan, grated
- ½ tsp salt
- n. B chili
- n. B garlic

FOR COVERING:

- 100 g   Mushrooms, brown
- 750 g   Spinach leaves (frozen)
- n. B salt

- n. B nutmeg
- n. B chili
- 6th Cherry tomato
- 1 ball Mozzarella, light
- 50 g Goat cheese

PREPARATION

1. For the pizza or casserole base, the lean ground beef (I have the butcher twist this twice from a roast), 1 tbsp mustard without sugar (please read the label), 2 eggs, 1/2 tsp salt, 2 tbsp grated Parmesan and Mix 4 teaspoons of macadamia nut flour. If you like it spicy, you can add chilli flakes to the mass. Then distribute the mixture evenly in a large baking dish.
2. Cut the brown mushrooms into slices, spread on the ground beef base and season with salt. Squeeze out the thawed spinach leaves so that it is not quite so wet and spread over the mushrooms. Salt and season with nutmeg and chilli flakes as desired. Cut the cherry tomatoes into slices and place on top. Cut the mozzarella and goat cheese into cubes and spread over the spinach.
3. Cook the spinach and minced meat casserole for approx. 45 minutes at 180 ° C convection / hot air in the preheated oven.

LOW CARB BACON EGG ROULE

Preparation time: 5 minutes

Cooking/Baking time: 10 minutes

Serving: 1

INGREDIENTS

- 3 Egg (s)
- 6 slice / n Bacon
- 25 ml Cream, optional
- 1 handful Mozzarella, grated
- 1 Avocado (s)

PREPARATION

1. Mash the avocado with a fork, season with salt and pepper and set aside. Fry the bacon in a large pan and set aside.
2. Whisk the eggs with the cream (you can also omit the cream) and add to the large pan, season with salt and pepper. Fry like an omelette, if there is still a liquid egg in the middle, it doesn't matter. Distribute the mozzarella and bacon evenly on top, place the bacon lengthways on the egg, then it can be rolled up more easily. Leave two slices for the topping. Roll it up and flatten it each time with the spatula until the whole egg is rolled up. Spread the mashed avocado and the rest of the bacon on the roll.
3. Of course, you can fill the bacon egg roule as you like. I still like cherry tomatoes and freshly chopped spring onions in them. The main thing is that the pan is nicely

greased so that the omelette slips nicely in the pan. You can also add the mozzarella directly to the eggs, but I like a liquid mozzarella core.

KETO RICE PUDDING

Preparation time: 5 minutes

Cooking/Baking time: 5 minutes

Serving: 1

INGREDIENTS

- 200 g Konja circle
- 200 ml milk
- 2 tbsp Erythritol (sugar substitute)
- ½ tsp Guar gum
- Flavdrops (vanilla flavor)
- Cinnamon powder

PREPARATION

1. Mix the milk with the guar gum. This works best with a milk frother. Then bring to the boil together with the konja circle and the erythritol.
2. Simmer for about 5 minutes until the desired consistency is reached. Season to taste with the flavdrops, cinnamon and erythritol. Tastes pure or with fresh berries.

LOW CARB PANCAKES

Preparation time: 15 minutes

Cooking/Baking time: 10 minutes

Serving: 1

INGREDIENTS

- 2 Egg (s)
- 100 g   cream cheese
- 25 g Soy flour
- n. B Sweeteners, e.g. flavdrops
- 50 g Berry

PREPARATION

1. The ingredients make 3 pancakes that fill you up well. First mix the eggs and cream cheese with the whisk of a hand mixer until no more lumps can be seen. Now slowly add the soy flour until it is completely stirred in. Finally, sweeten with a sweetener of your choice and stir, I prefer flavdrops and liquid sweetener.
2. If you would like to refine your pancakes with something sweet, you should now put about 50 g berries in a small saucepan over low heat with 2 tablespoons of water. As soon as the liquid boils, sweeten as needed.

3. Meanwhile, put the pancake batter in an oiled or greased, small, coated pan. Fry over medium to high heat until the dough is reasonably firm on top and turn once. Finally, pour the berry sauce over the pancakes and serve warm.

Preparation time: 6 minutes

Cooking/Baking time: 50 minutes

Serving: 4

INGREDIENTS

- 4th Beef steak (s)
- Oil for frying
- Salt and pepper from the mill

PREPARATION

1. Take the steaks out of the refrigerator 1 hour before preparation. Wash and pat dry the steaks.
2. Preheat the oven to 85 ° C top / bottom heat with a fire-proof dish (casserole dish) on the middle rack (gas: level 1).
3. Fry the steaks for 2 minutes on each side in hot oil. Season with salt and pepper. Then, place the baking dish in a preheated oven for 45 - 50 minutes at the same temperature.
4. Either heat the plates together with the ovenproof dish (baking dish) in the oven or heat them in the microwave.

SALMON CRUSTED WITH PARMESAN, HERBS, AND WALNUTS

Preparation time: 20 minutes
Cooking/Baking time: 25 minutes
Serving: 4

INGREDIENTS

- 800 g Salmon, with skin
- 1 Lemon (s), organic
- 1 Garlic cloves)
- 1 bunch Parsley smooth
- 1 branch / s sage
- 60 g Walnuts
- 40 g Parmesan, freshly grated
- 2 tbsp butter
- 250 g Whole milk yogurt
- some Sea salt and pepper, black from the mill

PREPARATION

1. Rinse the salmon, pat dry with kitchen paper, and use tweezers to remove any remaining bones. Rinse the lemon with hot water, rub dry and peel off the peel with a zest or peel off with a fine grater. Peel and finely chop the garlic. Rinse the parsley and sage, shake dry and chop together with the walnuts.

2. Mix the lemon peel, garlic, herbs, nuts, Parmesan, sea salt and pepper with 1 tbsp. Soft butter. Preheat the oven to 200 degrees (convection 180 degrees).

3. Place the salmon side on the skin in an oven-safe, buttered dish. Spread the herb-nut mixture evenly on top of the fish and lightly press with your hands. Put the pan in

the oven and bake the fish for about 25 minutes. Season the well-chilled yogurt with salt and pepper and serve with the salmon.

Made in the USA
Coppell, TX
01 February 2022